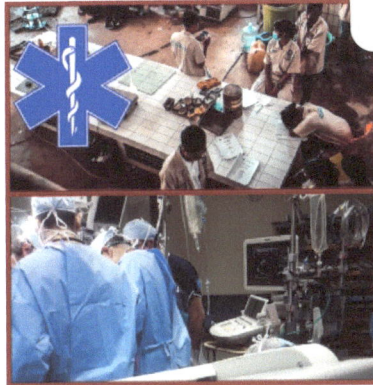

Quality Improvement in Healthcare Organizations

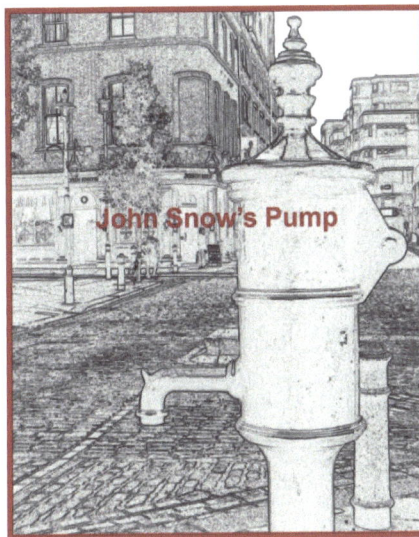

Note: The above picture is adapted from the picture found on Wikimedia Commons showing the John Snow Memorial in London (https://commons.wikimedia.org/wiki/File:John_Snow_memorial_and _pub.jpg)

About this Book

Some readers prefer a brief overview before reading a book. Others prefer no overview – they want to jump right into the book's content. Still others prefer a more thorough overview. If you prefer a brief overview, read on. If you wish to skip the overview and head immediately and directly to the content of the book, go to *Lesson One: Definition of Quality and Quality Improvement in Healthcare Organizations* or to *Lesson One Content and Discussion*. If you prefer a more detailed overview at this time, please see *Appendix A: Expanded Book Overview*. Appendix A is redundant with the information contained in this section. It is provided because some readers prefer a more detailed overview of the book than is provided in this section. The Table of Contents follows this brief overview section.

*****

Healthcare organization quality improvement (e.g., improvement in the quality of organizational functioning, improvement in the quality of health care delivery) requires an understanding of healthcare organization and delivery processes as well as ways to measure those processes. It requires understanding of statistical analyses which use those measures to decide if there has been quality improvement in those processes. It may seem cut-and-dry, but the history of the healthcare quality movement [bib#1] is full of drama.

For example, Ignaz Semmelweis [bib#2] proposed in 1847 that doctors should wash their hands with chlorinated lime solution to prevent the spread of disease and improve both health care and healthcare organization quality. His idea was rejected – continuously and soundly – and it is thought that this rejection led to his nervous breakdown and death in 1865.

About the same time (1854), John Snow [bib#3] (this is NOT the John Snow from the Game of Thrones) tried to improve the health quality of people drinking water from the London Broad Street Pump. His measurements and analysis led him to believe that water from the Broad Street Pump was the source of cholera in the area. People would not listen so he removed the handle of the Broad Street Pump [bib#4] so it could not be used. Being unable to convince the public and the government of the validity of his quality improvement analysis, he stopped the cholera outbreak with a wrench.

Ernest Codman, MD [bib#5] pioneered the use of quality standards for hospitals and doctors. Dr. Codman was a founding member of the American College of Surgeons (ACS) [bib#6] in 1912 and was instrumental in the formation of its Hospital Standardization program in 1917. However, not everyone was happy with these efforts. In fact, his insistence that the quality (competence) and outcomes of his surgical colleagues at Massachusetts General Hospital (MGH) be evaluated got him fired from MGH in 1914 [bib#7].

Florence Nightingale [bib#8] was a nurse in the Crimean War [bib#9] (1853 – 1856). While there she collected data on the deaths of soldiers for the purpose of analyzing the data to improve the quality of military hospitals to reduce soldier mortality. She organized that data into polar area diagrams (which she invented) to demonstrate that disease, especially disease from unsanitary conditions, was the primary cause of soldier deaths. Polar area diagrams are sometimes called coxcombs [bib#10].

As a result of this and other statistical work, Florence Nightingale was made a member of the International Statistical Institute (ISI) [bib#11], a Fellow of the Royal Statistical Society [bib#12] and an honorary member of the American Statistical Association [bib#13].

Perhaps you have thought about healthcare quality and ways it could be improved just as Ignaz Semmelweis, John Snow, Ernest Codman, and Florence Nightingale did. You may have asked yourself if there is a way for you to determine the relative quality of your healthcare choices? Have you found yourself thinking that there should be a way for you to provide your view and input on the quality of healthcare organization? Or do you work in a healthcare organization and find yourself thinking that there must be better ways to continuously and systematically improve the quality of your healthcare organization? If you have, this book is for you.

This book is an overview of quality and quality improvement programs, measures, and data in healthcare organizations. These topics are addressed from an evidence-based perspective. The evidence-based approach relies on data which are scientifically collected and analyzed using statistical techniques coupled with literature reviews. It is the foundational approach in modern health care quality improvement systems. The evidence-based approach is used as it helps inform and selects the best approaches (e.g., best treatment, best organizational structure, best quality measures). It is often referred to in this book.

This book is for those with a developing interest in the organizational operations, administration, and quality improvement in healthcare organizations and for those who have some expertise, but who wish an overview or refresher of these topics.

Unlike most other texts, this book has an agenda or purpose aimed at aiding the reader. The book knows that you have your own specific personal goals regarding quality improvement in healthcare organizations (e.g., improve your ability to facilitate the management of quality improvement in a healthcare organization, improve your healthcare administration skills, learn more about quality improvement programs in healthcare organizations in general). It also assumes that readers have different specific goals. The purpose of this book is to enable you to develop your own learning path to reach your learning goal regardless of what that goal happens to be. The intent of the book is to provide you with content and resources to pursue a personal learning path. That content extends past the reading of this text and will help you in your chosen work or study.

The unique purpose of the book requires a unique format. The format includes tons of resources (some would say encyclopedic) coupled with the Socratic Method and suggested competency development tasks. The Socratic Method promotes understanding of a topic by posing questions on that topic. Answering the question requires a learner/reader to think critically and synthesize information. The overall competency goal for all readers of this book is that it enables each reader to think more critically and more independently about quality improvement in healthcare organizations.

The book is organized into four (4) lessons. Each lesson is organized around competency objectives, questions, readings, competency development tasks (e.g., quiz) to organize your thinking and cement your learning. It is a format which makes extensive use of the resources available on the internet. As such the book provides links to external sites to connect you to the larger "*real world*" of healthcare organizations to help you better build your own learning path. The links also serve as resources you can use after you complete this book. Many might say that the most valuable part of this book is the list of resources provided for the reader.

These links (more than 575) are directly accessible in the content in the e-book version. For the print version – and for reference in the e-book version – the full URL for each link in the book can be found at the corresponding in-text link number [bib#] in the section at the end of the book entitled *Bibliography: Associated URL/Link List*. The list includes data, management, and research links needed for healthcare administration, management, and operations related to quality improvement in a healthcare organization.

The competency development tasks in this book facilitate content mastery to help you organize your thinking. Such organized thought should help you determine the relationship between the book content, a personal learning path, and achievement of personal goals. Competency development tasks in this book are: discussion questions, quizzes, and a project. Again, this is a Socratic approach in that the book asks for your thinking on the topics.

The included project is intended to help you synthesize content material by designing a quality improvement program of your choice for a healthcare organization of your choice the way you would have things run in the best of all worlds. The design is communicated in electronic spreadsheet format. An example of a completed spreadsheet project is found in *Appendix B: Spreadsheet Example*. The spreadsheet is an artifact which you can circulate to colleagues or use as the basis for a talk or presentation event. The philosophy behind this project is that more learning occurs – and learning is more fun – if you can actually build/create something from the content and it is useful beyond the reading of this book.

And because everyone loves a road trip/field trip, there are also "*virtual field trips*" to the often hidden places of interest on the web. There are also trivia questions – just for fun – because everyone also loves little known, but interesting, fun facts.

v

This book is dense in the physics sense of the word. There is a lot of detail we have to introduce to get people on the playing field. There is no royal road to acquiring that depth of information. We have attempted to organize the information and to make it searchable. One needs to take a break every so often to absorb the material. This is one of the reasons why virtual field trips and trivia questions are provided. Historical and social context is important in healthcare. Many of the links, virtual field trips, and trivia questions provide this context.

This book follows the content of and can be used as an adjunct to the Coursera course: *Quality Improvement in Care Delivery in Healthcare Organizations* found at https://www.coursera.org/learn/quality-improvement-in-healthcare-organizations. Should you prefer a learning experience which can result in an earned certificate or prefer a community of learners in the same course of study, consider enrolling in the Coursera course.

Note: The photograph shown at the beginning of this section is a composite of photos downloaded from Unsplash (https://unsplash.com/) by Natanael Melchor and Umari Bethan. The photographs used for the cover of the book were produced by Natanael Melchor, Umari Bethan, Tom Grimbert, and rawpixel (downloaded from Unsplash) as well as a photograph from Wikimedia Commons.

ISBN-13: 978-1-7336928-3-0

Imprint: Margaret Kilduff, Independent Publishing

Version 1.0, May 2020

Margaret Kilduff, Ph.D.

Professor Emerita

Rutgers University

Table of Contents

Lesson Four (L4): Design a Healthcare Organization Quality Improvement Program...141

Appendix A: Expanded Book Overview.................................163

Appendix B: Spreadsheet Example....................................175
Bibliography: Associated URL/Link List.............................185

Lesson One (L1): Definition of Quality and Quality Improvement in Healthcare Organizations

Note: The above picture is adapted from the one by Sarah Stierch found on Wikimedia Commons (https://commons.wikimedia.org/wiki/File:Department_of_Health_%26_Human_Services_-_Stierch.jpg)

L1 Competency Objective

This lesson provides an overview of the content in this book as well as an overview of quality and quality improvement in healthcare organizations. The competency objective is:

- Define quality and quality improvement in healthcare organizations

L1 Getting Started

L1 Welcome and Find Your Seat

The start of every learning path – the start of every course, every lesson, every targeted learning adventure – begins by "*finding your seat*". It begins by finding the location best suited for you to study and learn the targeted material. In today's world – in today's online information world – that "*seat*" can be in your kitchen, a coffee shop, on public transportation – anywhere there is an internet connection.

There is something nice, however, about finding a seat – even if only in your mind's eye – in a library, especially one of the iconic libraries. Such iconic libraries are architecturally stunning and provide a wonderful environment in which to ponder, consider, and learn. A few are shown below. Feel free to "*take a seat*" – any seat – in your mind's eye in one of them before moving on to the next sections.

Chicago Public Library [bib#14] (founded in 1873) especially the Winter Garden, Harold Washington Library [bib#15]

Image from Wikipedia, File:9th Level Harold Washington Library.jpg [bib#16]

Seattle Public Library [bib#17] (founded in 1890) especially the new Central Library [bib#18]

Image from Wikipedia, File:Seattle library main branch overhead.jpg

---

New York Public Library [bib#19] (founded in 1895) especially the Rose Main Reading Room, Stephen A. Schwarzman Building [bib#20]

Image from Wikipedia, File:NYC Public Library Research Room Jan 2006.jpg (Photo by DAVID ILIFF. License: CC-BY-SA 3.0) [bib#21]

L1 Discussion Question: Personal Learning Goal for this Learning Path

After finding your seat, it is often helpful to consider your personal learning goal for a learning path. Almost everyone has a personal learning goal at the beginning of every book, every course, every lesson, and every targeted learning adventure. Do you have a personal learning goal for this book? If so, what is it? Where do you want to be at the end of the learning path defined by this book? Where does this book fit into your personally chosen learning path which leads to achievement of personal goals?

L1 Content and Discussion

This lesson provides an overview of quality and quality improvement in healthcare organizations. Upon successful completion of this lesson, you will be able to: define quality and quality improvement in healthcare organizations. There are topic questions, a discussion question, a quiz, a trivia question, and a field trip. The lesson should take 4 - 6 hours of work to successfully complete. There are also videos which provide supplemental content which can help you better define your personal learning path. There are many wonderful videos in the public domain which are relevant to the topics in this book. One is listed immediately below.

*****

Video [bib#22]: *There are many wonderful videos in the public domain which are relevant to the topics in this book. Some of the videos highlight landmarks of high quality such as those listed as Historic Landmarks [bib#23]by the American Society of Civil Engineers (ASCE): "each of these engineering feats represents the achievement of what was considered an impossible dream".*

*One such video provides interesting information about the Golden Gate Bridge and the quality of its construction. The video – **What Do You Know About the Golden Gate Bridge?** – is a YouTube video produced by the Smithsonian Channel. The link for the video is:*
https://www.youtube.com/watch?v=6HygbD44_j4

*****

This lesson addresses five (5) topics organized as questions. An example answer is provided for each question. The purpose of the answer is to help you organize your thinking and come to your own conclusions and answer consistent with your personal learning goal. The questions/topics for Lesson One are:

1. What is the definition of quality and quality improvement in healthcare organizations?

2. What quality improvement frameworks and models are used in healthcare organizations?

3. What are the healthcare organization quality domains?

4. What are the organizations which encourage and support quality efforts in healthcare organizations?

5. What are the types of quality measures used for quality improvement in healthcare organizations?

L1 Topic 1 (T1). What is the definition of quality and quality improvement in healthcare organizations?

Before one can define quality improvement, the term "*quality*" has to be defined. This section addresses:

- Definition of Quality in Healthcare Organizations
- Definition of Quality Improvement in Healthcare Organizations

L1-T1. Definition of Quality in Healthcare Organizations

Merriam-Webster Dictionary defines quality [bib#24] as the "*degree of excellence*". The quality of an organization, therefore, is its degree of excellence. But there are many aspects to any organization and, therefore, many potential aspects of quality (e.g., products, customer service, facilities, business processes). Business Dictionary defines quality with respect to a manufacturing organization [bib#25] and defines quality as "*a measure of excellence or a state of being free from defects, deficiencies and significant variations ... in order to satisfy specific customer or user requirements".*

These definitions of quality are consistent with one of the most widely used definitions of health care quality [bib#26] which is the *"degree to which health services for individuals and populations increase the likelihood of desired health outcomes and are consistent with current professional knowledge".*

Combining aspects of all of the above definitions, a definition of healthcare organization quality **is:** *the degree to which the health care delivered by the healthcare organization consistently reflects current professional knowledge/standards while meeting the patient/customer personal health outcome expectations/requirements.*

It is important to note that sometimes the patient/customer expectations/requirements of a personal health outcome might not be met even if current professional knowledge/standards are met. In short, a patient/customer could receive high quality health care (free from defects, deficiencies and significant variations) and still be disappointed with the personal health outcome; still judge the health care as low quality. This is not an unusual situation in cosmetic surgery or health care delivered for the relief of chronic pain.

Sometimes patients/customers have unrealistic expectations/requirements of the personal health outcome. How patients/customers develop these unrealistic expectations/requirements is a subject of much discussion. Some blame the health care delivery professional (e.g., poor communication with the patient to explain reasonable expectations). Some blame the patient/consumer (e.g., not listening to the health care delivery professional's explanation of a reasonable expectation).

Sometimes, however, patients/customers do have realistic expectations/requirements which are not met because the health care is of low quality (contains defects, deficiencies and significant variations). Medical errors do occur, often with disastrous consequences. A Johns Hopkins study [bib#27], for example, estimates that 10 percent of all deaths in the United States each year result from a medical error; more than 250,000 deaths per year making medical errors and the third leading cause of death in the United States. Medical error [bib#28] is defined as:

> "*an unintended act (either of omission or commission) or one that does not achieve its intended outcome, the failure of a planned action to be completed as intended (an error of execution), the use of a wrong plan to achieve an aim (an error of planning), or a deviation from the process of care that may or may not cause harm to the patient*".

Some medical errors are medication errors. More than 100,000 suspected medication errors are reported every year to the United States Food and Drug Administration (FDA) via its MedWatch [bib#29] Safety Information and Adverse Event Reporting Program. A medication error [bib#30] is defined as:

> "*any preventable event that may cause or lead to inappropriate medication use or patient harm while the medication is in the control of the health care professional, patient, or consumer. Such events may be related to professional practice, health care products, procedures, and systems, including prescribing, order communication, product labeling, packaging, and nomenclature, compounding, dispensing, distribution, administration, education, monitoring, and use*".

It is estimated that an 700,000 emergency room visits and 100,000 hospitalizations every year result from an ADE.

*****

> ***Video*** [bib#31]***:*** *The video for Topic 1 – **MedWatch Tips & Tools** – is a YouTube video produced by the United States Food and Drug Administration (FDA). This video discusses how to use MedWatch to report a suspected or identified serious problem with a medical product. The link for the video is:* https://www.youtube.com/watch?v=7b-fcRQ2Q7k

*****

Often when patient/customer expectations/requirements of health care delivery from a healthcare organization are not met, the patient/customer files a medical malpractice claim [bib#32] against the healthcare organization. Approximately 17,000 medical malpractice [bib#33] claims are filed in the United States each year. It is estimated that [bib#34] 75% of physicians in low-risk specialties (e.g., family medicine) face a malpractice claim sometime in the course of their career while almost all of those physicians in high-risk specialties (e.g., neurosurgery) do.

Some people in the healthcare industry argue that the number of medical malpractice claims forces health care delivery professionals to practice defensive medicine. Defensive medicine [bib#35] is defined as a:

"*situation in which a doctor practices medicine, either through diagnosis or treatment, not to help the patient, but rather to prevent legal action ... if a problem occurs. The doctor goes beyond what is usually necessary for diagnosing and treating the patient so they can ensure they are not missing any unlikely but possible condition.*

They may perform procedures that the patient wants or expects even if they aren't clinically necessary, to keep the patient satisfied. For these reasons, defensive medicine is said to lead to overtesting and overtreatment. They want to prevent bad outcomes (however unlikely) and to prevent having an angry patient ...

Another aspect of defensive medicine is when a physician or medical practice avoids treating high-risk patients. They cherry-pick patients who are more likely to have good outcomes or they choose a medical specialty that has less risk of malpractice suits. This can result in the most talented doctors not treating the patients who need their skills the most."

It is estimated that the practice of defensive medicine [bib#36] adds $45 billion to the cost of healthcare in the United States each year.

Because of the time, effort, and money involved in defensive medicine, some argue that medical liability tort reform [bib#37] is needed. Medical liability tort reform legislation at the state-level (as opposed to federal-level) limits malpractice claims filed in that state. Such tort reform:

> "*usually includes laws that limit, or cap, the amount of money that patients can receive as an award from a clinician they've sued for malpractice. Additionally, tort reform caps the amount of punitive damages a judge can order the physician to pay. In some states, tort reform also puts tighter restrictions on medical malpractice suits to be tried in court, as opposed to dismissed or dropped.*"

More than half [bib#38] of the states have some sort of tort reform laws in effect. There is disagreement, however, as to whether such laws actually reduced overall healthcare expenditures.

It is important to note that value and cost are also intertwined with the concept of expectations/requirements – and thus cost and value are intertwined with the judgment of quality. Products/services must meet the customer/user expectations/requirements for the value given the cost. For example, customers/users might judge a 10 dollar plastic table which seats four of higher quality than a 100 dollar wood table which seats eight – if the plastic table was a very good buy for 10 dollars (a very, very good 10 dollar table) while the 100 dollar table was not such a good buy (not a great 100 dollar table; better 100 dollar tables exist). The plastic table might also be a very well made plastic table (being free from defects, deficiencies and significant variations) while the wood table is not a well made wood table. In short, higher cost does not necessarily mean higher value or higher quality.

L1-T1. Definition of Quality Improvement in Healthcare Organizations

Quality Improvement (QI) is a process to improve quality. QI in healthcare organizations is a process to improve healthcare organization quality. The Health Resources and Services Administration (HRSA) defines QI [bib#39] as the "*systematic and continuous actions that lead to measurable improvement in health care services and the health status of targeted patient groups*".

Incorporating the definition of quality from above and this definition of QI, a definition of quality improvement in healthcare organizations is the: *systematic and continuous actions that lead to measurable improvement healthcare organization quality; that is, systematic and continuous actions that lead to measurable improvement in the degree to which the health care delivered by the healthcare organization consistently reflects current professional knowledge/standards while meeting the patient/customer personal health outcome expectations/requirements.*

QI is a slightly different concept than Quality Assurance (QA) [bib#40]. QA is the process of ensuring that each and every organizational product and service meets the quality standard set for it; that is, a product/service of consistent quality is delivered each and every time. QI, on the other hand, is the process to continually improve the quality of the organization's products and services; that is, the product/service delivered next year is consistently of higher quality than the one delivered this year.

For successful QI, a healthcare organization must continually devote resources to a formal quality improvement program. QI is implemented through a formal quality improvement program which must be part of the organization's day-to-day operations. Such a QI program [bib#41] incorporates all of the systematic and continuous actions that lead to measurable improvement healthcare organization quality. HRSA states that all successful QI programs in healthcare organizations include a focus on:

- The operation of the healthcare organization as a system and sub-systems comprised of resources/inputs (e.g., health care delivery professionals), activities/processes (e.g., health care delivery actions), and outputs/outcomes (e.g., change in patient/customer health status).

- Patient/customer exceptions/requirements of the healthcare organization as a whole and, specifically, the health care delivered.

- The need for everyone in the healthcare organization to work as a team with a common goal of QI.

- Collecting and analyzing both qualitative and quantitative data to track quality.

L1 Topic 2 (T2). What quality improvement frameworks and models are used in healthcare organizations?

As stated in Topic 1, every Quality Improvement (QI) program includes a focus on:

- The operation of the healthcare organization as a system.
- Patient/customer exceptions/requirements.
- The need for everyone in the healthcare organization to work as a team.
- Collecting and analyzing both qualitative and quantitative data to track quality.

However, this focus can be implemented in many ways. These focus areas (characteristics) can be incorporated into a variety of different types of quality improvement frameworks and models. Using a defined framework to implement a quality improvement program provides a structure to ensure that the QI program involves the four focus areas and stays on track. This section discusses some of the quality improvement frameworks/models used in healthcare organizations.

Specifically, this section addresses:

- Chronic Care Model (CCM)
- Lean Framework
- Six Sigma Framework
- Lean Six Sigma Framework
- Model for Improvement (Plan-Do-Study-Act; PDSA)

L1-T2. Chronic Care Model (CCM)

The Chronic Care Model (CCM) [bib#42] is a QI framework/model to improve the quality of health care delivered to people with chronic illnesses/conditions. The model defines a chronic illness/condition as any illness/condition "*that requires ongoing adjustments by the affected person and interactions with the health care system*". The CCM is applicable to "*a variety of chronic illnesses, health care settings and target populations*" and identifies six aspects of quality care and improvement:

1. Health System [bib#43]: Create a culture, organization and mechanisms that promote safe, high quality care

2. Delivery System Design [bib#44]: Assure the delivery of effective, efficient clinical care and self-management support

3. Decision Support [bib#45]: Promote clinical care that is consistent with scientific evidence and patient preferences

4. Clinical Information Systems [bib#46]: Organize patient and population data to facilitate efficient and effective care

5. Self-Management Support [bib#47]: Empower and prepare patients to manage their health and health care

6. The Community [bib#48]: Mobilize community resources to meet needs of patients

L1-T2. Lean Framework

The Lean framework/model is directed toward maximizing what the patient/customer expects/requires in the most cost effective manner (e.g., eliminating waste). Use of the Lean Model [bib#49] in healthcare organizations "*empowers employees to speak up about problems affecting patient care, create patient-centered processes and work for the benefit of all patients every day*". The key aspects of Lean Health Care [bib#50] are:

- A healthcare organization-wide culture of continuous patient-centered quality improvement

- All healthcare organization processes are patient-centered; add value from the patient's perspective

- All healthcare organization personnel have a shared vision of quality improvement

- All healthcare organization personnel are given permission and the ability to initiate quality improvement actions

- The healthcare organization makes any and all indicated changes to improve quality

The Lean framework/model was not originally applied to healthcare organizations. It was applied to manufacturing and has its foundation in the Toyota Production System [bib#51] which was inspired by [bib#52] the manufacturing processes of Henry Ford [bib#53]. Best known of Ford's innovative manufacturing processes is the moving assembly line [bib#54].

In the Lean framework/model, cost-effectiveness focus is generally on eliminating waste in eight categories sometimes abbreviated as: TIM U WOOD.

- T: Transportation Waste (excessive, unnecessary transportation/movement of organizational people, products, information, customers, etc.)

- I: Inventory Excess/Waste (excessive, unnecessary storing of organizational inventory ahead of requirements)

- M: Motion Waste (excessive, unnecessary bending, turning, reaching, etc. by organizational personnel and customers)

- U: Unused Creativity (under-utilizing, and thus wasting, the skills, capabilities, and creativity of organizational personnel)

- W: Waiting Time (excessive, unnecessary waiting for organizational services, parts, information, etc. by personnel and customers; time wasting waiting unnecessarily)

- O: Over Processing Waste (using more material or doing more than is needed to accomplish the organizational task; thus, wasting resources)

- O: Over Production Waste (producing more products, making more, than is immediately required by the organization)

- D: Defects/Rework Waste (wasted time and effort to redo work done incorrectly)

*****

Video [bib#55]: *The video for Topic 2 – **The 8 Wastes in Health Care** – is a YouTube video produced by the University Health Network (UHN). This video discusses the eight TIM U WOOD Lean wastes found in health care. The link for the video is:* https://www.youtube.com/watch?v=7mA1L_a_FX4

*****

Some useful additional resources are:

- What is Lean Healthcare? [bib#56]
- Lean Principles in Healthcare: 2 Important Tools Organizations Must Have [bib#57]
- Lean Enterprise Institute [bib#58]
- Going Lean in Healthcare [bib#59]
- Lean [bib#60]
- Lean Management—The Journey from Toyota to Healthcare [bib#61]

L1-T2. Six Sigma Framework

The Six Sigma [bib#62] framework/model is directed toward reducing errors/defects within an organization. One example for a healthcare organization is reducing the number of medical errors which occur in that organization. An acceptable Six Sigma error rate [bib#63] is no greater than 0.000001, but the error rate in healthcare organizations is estimated to be, overall, the much higher 0.01 (unacceptable error rate). At the core of Six Sigma methodology are DMAIC and DMADV. DMAIC is a data-driven strategy used to reduce errors/defects by improving existing healthcare organization processes. DMADV is a data-driven strategy used to reduce errors/defects by developing new healthcare organization processes.

DMAIC [bib#64] stands for:

- Define the problem, improvement activity, opportunity for improvement, the project goals, and patient/customer (internal and external) expectations/requirements.

- Measure healthcare organization process performance.

- Analyze the healthcare organization process to determine root causes of variation, poor performance (defects such as medical errors).

- Improve healthcare organization process performance by addressing and eliminating the root causes.

- Control the improved healthcare organization process and future process performance.

DMADV [bib#65] stands for:

- Define the problem, improvement activity, opportunity for improvement, the project goals, and patient/customer (internal and external) expectations/requirements.

- <u>Measure</u> healthcare organization process performance.

- <u>Analyze</u> the healthcare organization process to determine root causes of variation, poor performance (defects such as medical errors).

- <u>Design</u> alternatives to the current healthcare organization process which addresses and eliminates the root causes.

- <u>Verify</u> that the new alternative meets all healthcare organization expectations/requirements

The Six Sigma framework/model was not originally applied to healthcare organizations. Six Sigma was developed at Motorola [bib#66] to improve manufacturing quality.

Some useful additional resources are:

- What is Six Sigma? [bib#67]
- About Six Sigma [bib#68]

L1-T2. Lean Six Sigma Framework

Many quality improvement professionals have merged the Lean and Six Sigma frameworks/models into one unified approach called Lean Six Sigma which is a framework/model which simultaneously focuses on both maximizing what the patient/customer expects/requires in the most cost effective manner (e.g., eliminating waste) and reducing errors/defects within an organization. The basic strategy of Lean Six Sigma is to first use the Lean strategy to eliminate waste and make the processes cost effective. Once that is accomplished, the Six Sigma DMAIC or DMADV strategy is used to reduce errors/defects in the Lean streamlined processes by either improving them or replacing them.

Some useful additional resources are:

- Lean Six Sigma Institute (LSSI) [bib#69]

- Lean Six Sigma in Healthcare [bib#70]
- The Applicability of Lean and Six Sigma Techniques to Clinical and Translational Research [bib#71]
- Lean and Six Sigma in Acute Care: A Systematic Review of Reviews [bib#72]
- Which Is Better for Engaging Health Care Staff: Lean or Six Sigma [bib#73]

L1-T2. Model for Improvement (Plan-Do-Study-Act; PDSA)

The Model for Improvement [bib#74] is used by the Institute for Healthcare Improvement [bib#75]) (IHI) to guide its quality improvement work. The Model was developed by the Associates in Process Improvement (API [bib#76]) and is "*a simple, yet powerful tool for accelerating improvement. This model is not meant to replace change models that organizations may already be using, but rather to accelerate improvement.*" The model contains three questions (which can be answered in any order) and a process of testing the changes: a Plan-Do-Study-Act (PDSA) cycle. The three questions are:

- Setting Aims [bib#77]: What are we trying to accomplish?

- Establishing Measures [bib#78]: How will we know that a change is an improvement?

- Selecting Changes [bib#79]: What change can we make that will result in improvement?

Testing the changes [bib#80] is done via Plan-Do-Study-Act (PDSA) cycle once the three questions have been asked and answered. The changes are tested in real-time in the real-work setting concurrent with existing work practices, but in such a way so as not to interfere with existing workflow. In short, changes are tested on a small scale and not implemented on a wide scale until the healthcare organization is sure that the changes are better than the existing situation. There are four steps in the testing cycle: 1) Plan, 2) Do, 3) Study, and 4) Act. The shorthand reference for this testing cycle is PDSA.

1. Plan: Plan the test or observation, including a plan for collecting data
2. Do: Try out the test on a small scale
3. Study: Set aside time to analyze the data and study the results
4. Act: Refine the change, based on what was learned from the test
   Some useful additional resources are:

- Institute for Healthcare Improvement (IHI) Model for Improvement [bib#81]

- Examples of PDSA Cycles for Quality Improvement Activities to Address Elements of the Chronic Care Model [bib#82]

- Example for Improving Diabetes Management using PDSA Cycle Process [bib#83]

L1 Topic 3 (T3). What are the healthcare organization quality domains?

As stated in Topic 1 and Topic 2, there are many healthcare organization quality improvement frameworks/models from which to choose to implement a Quality Improvement (QI) program (e.g., Lean, Six Sigma. Lean Six Sigma). Each framework/model incorporates the four focus areas needed for a successful QI program in a healthcare organization:

- The operation of the healthcare organization as a system.
- Patient/customer exceptions/requirements.
- The need for everyone in the healthcare organization to work as a team.
- Collecting and analyzing both qualitative and quantitative data to track quality.

The question now becomes: On which content areas (domains) of healthcare organization functioning should the QI program be focused? Is there a way to organize healthcare organization thinking about the general sub-systems of organizational functioning for quality improvement?

This section addresses:

- Overview of Healthcare Organization Quality Domains
- Safety Quality Domain
- Effectiveness Quality Domain
- Person-Centeredness Quality Domain
- Accessibility, Timeliness, Affordability Quality Domain
- Efficiency Quality Domain
- Equity Quality Domain

L1-T3. Overview of Healthcare Organization Quality Domains

One of the most commonly used lists of quality domains for healthcare organizations is the one in the 2018 report entitled *Crossing the Global Quality Chasm: Improving Health Care Worldwide* [bib#84] which was published by National Academies of Sciences, Engineering, and Medicine; Health and Medicine Division [bib#85]; Board on Global Health [bib#86]; Board on Health Care Services [bib#87]; Committee on Improving the Quality of Health Care Globally [bib#88]. This report builds on the iconic 2001 Institute of Medicine (IOM) report entitled *Crossing the Quality Chasm: A New Health System for the 21st Century* [bib#89]

The IOM was renamed the National Academy of Medicine (NAM) in 2015. It is one of the three academies of the National Academies [bib#90] whose purpose is to [bib#91] "*provide independent, objective analysis and advice to the nation and conduct other activities to solve complex problems and inform public policy decisions*".

The first National Academy was the National Academy of Sciences (NAS), whose incorporation was signed into law [bib#92] by Abraham Lincoln in 1863. In 1964, the NAS established the National Academy of Engineering (NAE [bib#93]). The National Academy of Medicine (NAM) was founded in 1970 [bib#94] as the Institute of Medicine (IOM).

Research to provide objective analysis mentioned in the mission of the National Academies is done collectively by members of the three academies via the National Research Council (NRC [bib#95]). Studies and reports [bib#96] from the National Academies via the NRC "*on science policy, health and medicine, engineering and technology, education, and the environment often raise awareness about important issues and drive public policy decisions for many years after they are released.*" The NRC currently has seven program [bib#97] units including the Health and Medicine Division (HMD [bib#98]) which addresses topic areas such as Quality and Patient Safety [bib#99].

The quality domains listed as the Six Dimensions of Health Care Quality in *Crossing the Global Quality Chasm: Improving Health Care Worldwide* [bib#84], are:

1. Safety
2. Effectiveness
3. Person-Centeredness
4. Accessibility, Timeliness, Affordability
5. Efficiency
6. Equity

Although they are listed as dimensions/domains of Health Care Quality, they can also be considered dimensions/domains of Healthcare Organization Quality. Each one is discussed in the following sections.

L1-T3. Safety Quality Domain

The healthcare organization safety quality domain involves ensuring that patients in the healthcare organization are not harmed by the health care intended to help them.

The first step in Safety Quality Domain quality improvement (QI) is choosing the framework/model to use (e.g., Lean, Six Sigma). In Six Sigma language, improving patient/customer safety is similar to reducing organizational product defects/errors. However, regardless of the framework/model chosen, the QI process involves:

- Viewing the healthcare organization as a system within which is a sub-system of processes related to ensuring patient safety quality. Within that safety quality system, which cuts across the entire healthcare organization, are subsystems such as safety quality in surgery and safety quality in the intensive care unit (ICU).

- Understanding and respecting the patient/customer expectations/requirements of safety quality when interacting with the healthcare organization.

- Ensuring that all personnel in the healthcare organization work as a team to improve safety quality.

- Collecting and analyzing both qualitative and quantitative data to track safety quality across the entire healthcare organization.

One of the popular methods of attempting to ensure that all personnel in the healthcare organization work as a team to improve safety quality is TeamSTEPPS [bib#100] (Team Strategies and Tools to Enhance Performance and Patient Safety). TeamSTEPPS "*is an evidence-based set of teamwork tools, aimed at optimizing patient outcomes by improving communication and teamwork skills among health care professionals*".

*****

Video [bib#101]*: The video for Topic 3 – **Successful Outcome Using TeamSTEPPS Techniques** – is a YouTube video produced by the Agency for Healthcare Research and Quality (AHRQ). This video discusses TeamSTEPPS techniques which can lead to more successful patient outcomes. The link for the video is:*
https://www.youtube.com/watch?v=yWd56QVL1VQ

*****

One of the most important activities that a healthcare organization can easily undertake to improve patient safety quality is hand hygiene; that is, ensuring that hand washing protocols for personnel, patients, and visitors are followed. Clean hands [bib#102] reduce the probably of the occurrence of healthcare-associated infections (HAI [bib#103]). Every day, about one in 31 hospital patients [bib#104] has at least one healthcare-associated infection.

Ignaz Semmelweis [bib#2] is credited with being the first person to recognize the importance of hand washing to prevent infection. In 1847, he proposed that doctors wash their hands with chlorinated lime solution to prevent "*childbed fever*" (puerperal fever [bib#105]) in the Vienna General Hospital obstetrical unit. His colleagues, and most of the medical community at large, rejected his idea. He believed so fervently in his idea, and had collected some data to support it, that its continual rejection is said to have driven him to a nervous breakdown in 1865. He was committed to an asylum and died less than two weeks later of an infection [bib#106] resulting from a beating inflicted upon him in the asylum.

This situation led to the coining of the term "*Semmelweis Reflex*" [bib#107] sometimes called the "*Semmelweis Effect*" to describe the reflex-like tendency some people have to reject new evidence or new knowledge without further discussion or consideration because it contradicts established norms, beliefs or paradigms.

L1-T3. Effectiveness Quality Domain

The healthcare organization effective**ss** quality domain involves ensuring that healthcare organization patients/customers are provided with the optimal care for their situation; that is, they are provided with evidence-based health care which does not underuse appropriate, effective care and does not overuse ineffective, inappropriate care. The benefits of any health care outweigh any risks and the health care is clinically effective.

Many believe that Clinical Decision Support [bib#108] systems can improve the quality of clinical effectiveness. Clinical decision support (CDS [bib#109]) "*provides clinicians, staff, patients or other individuals with knowledge and person-specific information, intelligently filtered or presented at appropriate times, to enhance health and health care*".

The first step in Effectiveness Quality Domain quality improvement (QI) is choosing the framework/model to use (e.g., Lean, Six Sigma). Regardless of the framework/model chosen, the QI process involves:

- Viewing the healthcare organization as a system within which is a sub-system of processes related to ensuring effectiveness quality in health care (quality clinical effectiveness). Within that clinical effectiveness quality system, which cuts across the entire healthcare organization, are subsystems such as clinical effectiveness quality in surgery and clinical effectiveness quality in the intensive care unit (ICU).

- Understanding and respecting the patient/customer expectations/requirements of clinical effectiveness quality when interacting with the healthcare organization.

- Ensuring that all personnel in the healthcare organization work as a team to improve clinical effectiveness quality.

- Collecting and analyzing both qualitative and quantitative data to track clinical effectiveness quality across the entire healthcare organization.

L1-T3. Person-Centeredness Quality Domain

The healthcare organization person-centeredness quality domain involves ensuring that delivered health care in the healthcare organization is person/patient-centered; that is, each person is treated as an individual and that individual's wishes, preferences, needs, and values are respected and incorporated into health care delivery.

Whether delivered health care is truly person-centered can only be determined from the person/patient perspective. In short, it makes little difference what the health care professionals think about whether the health care is person-centered. The only one who can determine that and its quality is each and every individual person/patient who received care. Only the person's/patient's perspective matters.

The first step in Person-Centeredness Quality Domain quality improvement (QI) is choosing the framework/model to use (e.g., Lean, Six Sigma). Regardless of the framework/model chosen, the QI process involves:

- Viewing the healthcare organization as a system within which is a sub-system of processes related to ensuring person-centeredness quality. Within that person-centeredness quality system, which cuts across the entire healthcare organization, are subsystems such as person-centeredness quality in surgery and person-centeredness quality in the intensive care unit (ICU).

- Understanding and respecting the patient/customer expectations/requirements of person-centeredness quality when interacting with the healthcare organization.

- Ensuring that all personnel in the healthcare organization work as a team to improve person-centeredness quality.

- Collecting and analyzing both qualitative and quantitative data to track person-centeredness quality across the entire healthcare organization.

L1-T3. Accessibility, Timeliness, Affordability Quality Domain

The healthcare organization accessibility, timeliness, affordability quality domain involves ensuring that: 1) there are no unnecessary barriers to health care access at the healthcare organization; 2) healthcare organization wait times are optimized for both patients/customers and healthcare personnel (e.g., no unnecessary waiting); and 3) health care at the healthcare organization is as affordable as is possible.

Accessibility (access to care) quality and affordability quality are concerns not only for each individual healthcare organization, but also for the healthcare industry as a whole. For example, Healthy People 2020 [bib#110] has Access to Health Services [bib#111] as one of its topic areas. National health expenditures [bib#112] are more than three trillion dollars annually and expected to grow by five percent per year. Each healthcare organization can only improve accessibility quality and affordability quality within the constraints of quality of the healthcare industry as a whole (e.g., within current healthcare policy, within current healthcare insurance).

An individual healthcare organization has more control over timeliness quality than either accessibility quality or affordability quality in that healthcare organization. Timeliness references wait times, and the longer the wait time the lower the quality. There are many different types of timeliness (wait times) of concern to a healthcare organization. Some of them are:

- *Appointment Timeliness/Wait Time:* The amount of time that elapses between the time a patient makes contact with a healthcare provider for the purpose of scheduling an appointment and the time that appointment occurs.

- *Scheduled Appointment Waiting Room Timeliness/Wait Time:* The amount of time that elapses between the time of a patient's scheduled appointment with a healthcare provider and the time that patient is seen by a healthcare provider (time the scheduled appointment begins).

- *Test Results Timeliness/Wait Time:* The amount of time that elapses between the time a healthcare provider orders a test for a patient and the time the results of that patient's test are received by the healthcare provider who ordered the test.

- *Diagnosis Timeliness/Wait Time:* The amount of time that elapses between the time that a patient's symptoms are first noted by a healthcare provider and the time an accurate diagnosis is made for that patient's condition.

- *Visit Timeliness/Wait Time:* The amount of time a patient spends in an examination or treatment room after the start of an appointment without being seen by a healthcare provider.

- *Unscheduled Appointment Waiting Room Timeliness/Wait Time:* The amount of time that elapses between the time a patient checks in for an unscheduled appointment with a healthcare provider and the time that patient is seen by a healthcare provider (time the unscheduled appointment begins).

The first step in Accessibility, Timeliness, Affordability Quality Domain quality improvement (QI) is choosing the framework/model to use (e.g., Lean, Six Sigma. Regardless of the framework/model chosen, the QI process involves:

- Viewing the healthcare organization as a system within which is a sub-system of processes related to ensuring Accessibility, Timeliness, Affordability quality. Within that Accessibility, Timeliness, Affordability quality system, which cuts across the entire healthcare organization, are subsystems such as Accessibility, Timeliness, Affordability quality in surgery and Accessibility, Timeliness, Affordability quality in the intensive care unit (ICU).

- Understanding and respecting the patient/customer expectations/requirements of Accessibility, Timeliness, Affordability quality when interacting with the healthcare organization.

- Ensuring that all personnel in the healthcare organization work as a team to improve Accessibility, Timeliness, Affordability quality.

- Collecting and analyzing both qualitative and quantitative data to track Accessibility, Timeliness, Affordability quality across the entire healthcare organization.

L1-T3. *Efficiency Quality Domain*

The healthcare organization efficiency quality domain involves ensuring that processes in the healthcare organization are efficient; waste is eliminated. The first step in Efficiency Quality Domain quality improvement

(QI) is choosing the framework/model to use (e.g., Lean, Six Sigma). The Lean framework/model has as its primary focus the elimination of waste in organizational processes. Regardless of the framework/model chosen, the QI process involves:

- Viewing the healthcare organization as a system within which is a sub-system of processes related to ensuring efficiency quality. Within that efficiency quality system, which cuts across the entire healthcare organization, are subsystems such as efficiency quality in surgery and efficiency quality in the intensive care unit (ICU).

- Understanding and respecting the patient/customer expectations/requirements of efficiency quality when interacting with the healthcare organization.

- Ensuring that all personnel in the healthcare organization work as a team to improve efficiency quality.

- Collecting and analyzing both qualitative and quantitative data to track efficiency quality across the entire healthcare organization.

L1-T3. Equity Quality Domain

The healthcare organization equity quality domain involves ensuring that none of the other quality domains (e.g., safety, person-centeredness, timeliness) vary in quality with respect to a patient's/customer's personal characteristics (e.g., gender, ethnicity, race, age, disability status, socioeconomic status). Although an individual healthcare organization can address this issue fully within the organization's functioning, it is a concern of the healthcare industry as a whole. For example, Healthy People 2020 [bib#110] has an interest area [bib#113] ensuring that the Healthy People 2020 outcomes measure evidence of equity. Healthy People 2020 defines health equity as the:

> "*attainment of the highest level of health for all people. Achieving health equity requires valuing everyone equally with focused and*

ongoing societal efforts to address avoidable inequalities, historical and contemporary injustices, and the elimination of health and health care disparities".

Healthy People 2020 defines a health disparity as:

"*a particular type of health difference that is closely linked with social, economic, and/or environmental disadvantage. Health disparities adversely affect groups of people who have systematically experienced greater obstacles to health based on their racial or ethnic group; religion; socioeconomic status; gender; age; mental health; cognitive, sensory, or physical disability; sexual orientation or gender identity; geographic location; or other characteristics historically linked to discrimination or exclusion.*"

The first step in Equity Quality Domain quality improvement (QI) is choosing the framework/model to use (e.g., Lean, Six Sigma). Regardless of the framework/model chosen, the QI process involves:

- Viewing the healthcare organization as a system within which is a sub-system of processes related to ensuring equity quality. Within that equity quality system, which cuts across the entire healthcare organization, are subsystems such as equity quality in surgery and equity quality in the intensive care unit (ICU).

- Understanding and respecting the patient/customer expectations/requirements of equity quality when interacting with the healthcare organization.

- Ensuring that all personnel in the healthcare organization work as a team to improve equity quality.

- Collecting and analyzing both qualitative and quantitative data to track equity quality across the entire healthcare organization.

L1 Topic 4 (T4). What are the organizations which encourage and support quality efforts in healthcare organizations?

There are many organizations which focus some or all of their activity on encouraging organizations to include quality and quality improvement activities in their daily processes. Such organizations encourage and support the concept of organizational quality and often provide resources to support quality efforts in organizations.

Some focus on organizational quality and quality improvement in many industries (including healthcare). Some focus on only on the healthcare industry, on healthcare organizations. This section discusses some of these organizations. Specifically, this section addresses:

- Organizations which Encourage and Support Quality Efforts with a Multi-Industry Focus

- Organizations which Encourage and Support Quality Efforts with a Healthcare Organization Focus

L1-T4. Organizations which Encourage and Support Quality Efforts with a Multi-Industry Focus

Two of the more commonly known organizations which encourage and support quality efforts with a multi-industry focus are the:

1. National Institute of Standards and Technology (NIST [bib#114])
2. American Society for Quality (ASQ [bib#115])

National Institute of Standards and Technology (NIST [bib#114])

NIST, which was founded as the Bureau of Standards in 1901 [bib#116], provides quality resources for organizations via its development of measures and standards as well as its Baldrige Performance Excellence Program [bib#117]. The NIST motto is: "*MEASURE. INNOVATE. LEAD. Working with industry and science to advance innovation and improve quality of life.*"

The encouragement and support of quality in healthcare organizations is the focus of the NIST Health and Bioscience Division [bib#118] where "*research, calibrations, and standards development leadership help medical researchers and manufacturers of diagnostics and treatments be able to efficiently develop new products, and ensure efficacy and safety of treatments.*"

One responsibility of this Division is Health and Biological Systems Measurement [bib#119]. One quality contribution of this Division is the measurement information to eliminate vaccine waste. Measurement guidelines on vaccine storage [bib#120] were developed because as "*much as 35 percent of vaccines shipped worldwide is wasted because it is transported or stored at temperatures too high or too low. NIST's research ... recommend effective ways for vaccine providers to protect their vaccines and reduce waste*".

The NIST Baldrige Performance Excellence Program [bib#117] provides many quality resources including organizational self-assessment tools (called the Baldrige Excellence Framework [bib#121]) to help organizations organize their thinking and processes when implementing any quality improvement program. The Framework helps organizations identify areas within an organization which need improvement and it is often used in conjunction with Quality Improvement (QI) frameworks/models (e.g., Lean, Six Sigma) to make those improvements.

Although the Framework can be applied to an organization in any industry, NIST provides information specific for some industries such as Health Care [bib#122]. The Baldrige Excellence Framework (Health Care) and its Criteria [bib#123] are intended to help a healthcare organization manage the organization "*as a unified whole, so that ... plans, processes, measures, and actions are consistent*". Self-assessment improvement tools [bib#124] are provided as part of the Framework. One example is the *easyInsight: Take a First Step toward a Baldrige Self-Assessment For Health Care Organizations* [bib#125]

30

Another component of the Baldrige Performance Excellence Program is the annual Malcolm Baldrige National Quality Award [bib#126] which "*is the highest level of national recognition for performance excellence that a U.S. organization can receive ... Organizations don't receive the award for specific products or services. To receive the award, an organization must have a system that*

- *ensures continuous improvement in overall performance in delivering products and/or services*

- *provides an approach for satisfying and responding to customers and stakeholders*"

The awards are given by industry sector. One award sector is Health Care [bib#127]. Recent healthcare organization award recipients include Memorial Hospital and Health Care Center [bib#128] in Indiana, Adventist Health Castle [bib#129] in Hawaii, and Southcentral Foundation [bib#130] in Alaska.

The American Society for Quality (ASQ [bib#115])

ASQ has "*individual and organizational members around the world ... the reputation and reach to bring together the diverse quality champions who are transforming the world's corporations, organizations and communities to meet tomorrow's critical challenges*". ASQ administers [bib#131] the Malcolm Baldrige National Quality Award for NIST which manages the award. ASQ also supports quality in organizations in a number of additional ways such as:

- Publishing journals [bib#132] with a focus on organizational quality; the flagship journal is *Quality Progress* [bib#133]

- Quality Resources [bib#134] which is a "*one-stop online library of information related to quality. Access 70 years' worth of content for all experience levels*"

- [Professional certifications](#) [bib#135] such as Quality Auditor ([CQA](#) [bib#136]), Biomedical Auditor ([CBA](#) [bib#137]), and Pharmaceutical Good Manufacturing Practices (GMP) Professional ([CPGP](#) [bib#138])

*****

Video [bib#139]*: The video for Topic 4 – **ASQ TV Episode 2: Culture of Quality** – is a YouTube video produced by the American Society for Quality (ASQ). This video is an overview of the components of a culture of quality in an organization and its importance. The link for the video is:*
https://www.youtube.com/watch?v=VsSk_S226HM

*****

L1-T4. Organizations which Encourage and Support Quality Efforts with a Healthcare Organization Focus

Nine of the more commonly known organizations which encourage and support quality efforts with a healthcare organization focus are:

1. Agency for Healthcare Research and Quality ([AHRQ](#) [bib#140])
2. Institute for Healthcare Improvement ([IHI](#) [bib#141])
3. National Committee for Quality Assurance ([NCQA](#) [bib#142])
4. National Association for Healthcare Quality ([NAHQ](#) [bib#143])
5. Public Health Foundation ([PHF](#) [bib#144])
6. National Association of County and City Health Officials ([NACCHO](#) [bib#145])
7. Pharmacy Quality Alliance ([PQA](#) [bib#146])
8. The Centers for Medicare and Medicaid Services ([CMS](#) [bib#147])
9. Food and Drug Administration ([FDA](#) [bib#148])

Agency for Healthcare Research and Quality ([AHRQ](#) [bib#140])

AHRQ "*is the lead Federal agency charged with improving the safety and quality of America's health care system. AHRQ develops the knowledge, tools, and data needed to improve the health care system and help Americans, health care professionals, and policymakers make informed health decisions.*"

Some of the AHRQ resources useful to healthcare organization quality and quality improvement efforts are its "*range of data resources in online, searchable databases*" at its Data [bib#149] website as well as "*practical, research-based tools and other resources to help a variety of health care organizations, providers, and others make care safer in all health care settings*" at its Tools [bib#150] website.

Institute for Healthcare Improvement (IHI [bib#141])

IHI's mission is to "*improve health and health care worldwide*". IHI provides resources for the Model for Improvement [bib#74] which is "*a simple, yet powerful tool for accelerating improvement. This model is not meant to replace change models that organizations may already be using, but rather to accelerate improvement.*" IHI also offers professional certification, specifically the Certified Professional in Patient Safety (CPPS [bib#151]).

National Committee for Quality Assurance (NCQA [bib#142])

NCQA "*exists to improve the quality of health care ... better health care, better choices and better health*". They provide a number of resources to healthcare organizations interested in quality improvement. These include the Physician and Hospital Quality Certification [bib#152] for hospitals as well as the Quality Talks [bib#153] annual conference.

NCQA is also responsible for the Healthcare Effectiveness Data and Information Set (HEDIS [bib#154]) which "*is one of health care's most widely used performance improvement tools. 184 million people are enrolled in plans that report HEDIS results*". HEDIS data allow the comparison of health insurance plan performance to other health insurance plans and to benchmarks.

National Association for Healthcare Quality (NAHQ [bib#143])

NAHQ is "*the only organization dedicated to healthcare quality professionals*". NAHQ sponsors Healthcare Quality Week [bib#155] to celebrate "*the contributions professionals have made to improve healthcare quality*" and the Healthcare Quality Foundation (HQF [bib#156]) which "*promotes the continued advancement of the healthcare quality profession by supporting research and development, education, and related activities*". NAHQ also offers the Certified Professional in Healthcare Quality (CPHQ [bib#157]) credential which is the "*only accredited certification in the field of healthcare quality*".

Public Health Foundation (PHF [bib#144])

PHF has as one of its focus areas Quality Improvement in Public Health [bib#158] which is "*the use of a deliberate and defined improvement process, such as Plan-Do-Check-Act, which is focused on activities that are responsive to community needs and improving population health. It refers to a continuous and ongoing effort to achieve measureable improvements in the efficiency, effectiveness, performance, accountability, outcomes, and other indicators of quality in services or processes which achieve equity and improve the health of the community*". PHF provides many Quality Improvement Resources [bib#159] such as the QI Quick Guide [bib#160] and the Quality Improvement Tools [bib#161] to Advance Public Health Performance.

National Association of County and City Health Officials (NACCHO [bib#145])

NACCHO has a focus area on Quality Improvement [bib#162] because "*Quality improvement (QI) has been introduced to, and embraced by, the field of public health as a means to achieve efficiencies and improve quality of services to improve overall community health*".

Pharmacy Quality Alliance (PQA [bib#146])

PQA aims to advance the "*quality of medication use*". PQA has developed performance measures [bib#163] and encourages quality improvement in healthcare organizations through its Quality Forum Series [bib#164] and Quality Awards [bib#165] which recognize "*prescription drug plans that have high achievement or significant improvement in PQA measures of medication safety and appropriate use*".

The Centers for Medicare and Medicaid Services (CMS [bib#147])

CMS sponsors a number of Quality Initiatives [bib#166] which "*touch every aspect of the healthcare system*". The CMS Quality Strategy is based in the Meaningful Measures Framework [bib#167] which "*identifies high priority areas for quality measurement and improvement. Its purpose is to improve outcomes for patients, their families and providers while also reducing burden on clinicians and providers*".

Food and Drug Administration (FDA [bib#148])

The FDA has a number of quality initiatives/programs to ensure that healthcare organizations producing FDA-regulated products maintain quality in the process [bib#168]. One such initiative is the Quality System (QS) Regulation/Medical Device Good Manufacturing Practices [bib#169]. Another is Pharmaceutical Quality Resources [bib#170]. The FDA Center for Devices and Radiological Health (CDRH) itself has a quality improvement program for its own operations called the CDRH Quality Management Program [bib#171].

L1 Topic 5 (T5). What are the types of quality measures used for quality improvement in healthcare organizations?

All discussions of quality and quality improvement involve discussions of data. To improve something – anything – you need to be able to measure it. You need data (from measurements) on what the current situation is (what the current quality is) and data (from measurements) on what the quality becomes (data on quality improvement). Measurements, data, and ways to analyze that data for the purpose of quality improvement are discussed in more detail in Lesson Two and Lesson Three. This section discusses the general types of quality measures which produce data for quality improvement in healthcare organizations.

Specifically, this section addresses:

- Overview of Quality Measures
- Structural Quality Measures
- Process Quality Measures
- Outcome Quality Measures
- Characteristics of a Good Quality Measure

L1-T5. Overview of Quality Measures

The Centers for Medicare and Medicaid Services (CMS) defines Quality Measures [bib#172] as:

"*tools that help us measure or quantify healthcare processes, outcomes, patient perceptions, and organizational structure and/or systems that are associated with the ability to provide high-quality health care and/or that relate to one or more quality goals for health care. These goals include: effective, safe, efficient, patient-centered, equitable, and timely care ... CMS uses quality measures in its quality improvement, public reporting, and pay-for-reporting programs for specific healthcare providers*".

The Agency for Healthcare Research and Quality (AHRQ) defines Quality Measures as measures [bib#173] "*used to assess and compare the quality of health care organizations*".

When speaking of quality measures in the healthcare industry, most people organize the measures into three categories: 1) Structural Quality Measures, 2) Process Quality Measures, and 3) Outcome Quality Measures. This categorization is usually referred to as the Structure-Process-Outcome (SPO) Model or the Donabedian Model [bib#174]. It is named for Avedis Donabedian [bib#175] who is credited with the development of the SPO model and which he first published in his 1966 article entitled "Evaluating the quality of medical care" [bib#176]..

L1-T5. Structural Quality Measures

Structural Quality Measures are those related to the healthcare organization's structure. Such measures describe the healthcare organization itself. They describe the capacity of the healthcare organization's infrastructure. This infrastructure is comprised of physical facilities, personnel, and equipment. Examples include building square footage, number of board-certified physicians, number of beds, number and types of clinical departments, and hours of operation.

An advantage of structural measures is that they are relatively easy to obtain. A disadvantage of structural measures is that they do not really contain much functional information about a healthcare organization. For example, two healthcare facilities with the same square footage may not be equally efficient and effective in utilizing that square footage. They may not be the same in the way they functionally use that space (e.g., one may dedicate more space to waiting areas than another). In addition, the square footage may not be equally well maintained. The square footage of one healthcare organization may be perfectly maintained while the square footage in the other, although in use, is in need of extensive repair.

L1-T5. Process Quality Measures

Process Quality Measures are those related to the healthcare organization's processes. Such measures describe what happens in the healthcare organization. They describe what a patient can expect to encounter in the healthcare organization. These include not only the steps involved in a specific process, but also whether a process was delivered/offered to a patient. Examples of the former case include the check-in process (e.g., steps involved in check-in) and treatment processes (e.g., steps involved in the treatment of a broken leg). An example of the latter is whether the healthcare patient/consumer with diabetes was given diabetes education material and whether certain prevention/wellness procedures were offered (e.g., flu shot).

An advantage of process measures is that they are somewhat easy to identify and obtain. A disadvantage of process measures is that it is nearly impossible to measure all components of process measures. Choices regarding which to measure must be made and the components most important for quality are not necessarily obvious. In addition, there are often multiple acceptable processes (e.g., multiple acceptable treatment options) and measurement of the components might not be the same across all acceptable processes.

Another disadvantage of process measures is that they do not really contain much functional information about a healthcare organization. For example, two healthcare facilities which offer prevention/wellness procedures (e.g., flu shot) to healthcare patients/consumers might present that information in very different ways (e.g., one gives the patient/customer a flyer while another discusses the flu shot directly with the patient/consumer). They are not the same in the way they functionally offer the prevention/wellness procedure.

L1-T5. Outcome Quality Measures

Outcome Quality Measures are those related to the outcome (effect) of the healthcare organization's structure and process. In this sense, both Structural Quality Measures and Process Quality Measures should affect the Outcome Quality Measures. Of the three measure types (structural, process, outcome), Outcome Quality Measures are usually considered to be the most important – the "*gold standard*" of quality measures and are the ones usually publicly reported. The World Health Organization (WHO) defines such an outcome measure [bib#177] as a: "*change in the health status of an individual, group or population which is attributable to a planned intervention or series of* *intervention*s". Examples include patient/customer mortality and satisfaction with the healthcare organization.

One challenge with Outcome Quality Measures is the fact that the healthcare organization's structure and processes are not the only features in any patient's/customer's life. It is difficult to attribute any outcome (and change in health status) specifically to the healthcare organization. A patient/customer could fall and break some bones at home just after leaving a healthcare organization; it would seem unreasonable to attribute the fall and the fractures to the structure and processes of the healthcare organization. The other challenge is determining at what time period to obtain the Outcome Quality Measure data. For example, should it be measured at the moment a person leaves the healthcare organization, a day later, a week later, ...?

The first use of Outcome Quality Measures in health care is generally considered to be by Pierre-Charles-Alexandre Louis [bib#178] and his evaluation of the outcome of blood-letting [bib#179] as a treatment for pneumonia which was published in the 1835 work entitled *Researches On The Effects Of Bloodletting In Some Inflammatory Diseases* [bib#180]. Louis is sometimes described as the "*inventor of the numerical method in medicine*" [bib#181].

*****

> ***Video*** [bib#182]***:*** *The video for Topic 5 –* ***Outcome measures: Attributing a score*** *– is a YouTube video produced by the Wellington Medical and Health Sciences Library (WMHSLibrary). This video is A brief introduction to the different types of scores used to measure health outcomes. The link for the video is:*
> https://www.youtube.com/watch?v=1pnC7W93YeY

*****

L1-T5. Characteristics of a Good Quality Measure

Regardless of whether a quality measure is structural, process, or outcome, a good healthcare quality measure meets certain criteria (has specific characteristics). One of the best criteria lists is the one developed and used by the National Quality Forum (NQF [bib#183]) whose "*measures and standards serve as a critically important foundation for initiatives to enhance healthcare value, make patient care safer, and achieve better outcomes*". NQF was founded in 1999 and is the:

> "*only consensus-based healthcare organization in the nation as defined by the Office of Management and Budget. This status allows the federal government to rely on NQF-defined measures or healthcare practices as the best, evidence-based approaches to improving care*".

The NQF Measure Evaluation Criteria [bib#184] include:

1. Importance to Measure and Report: Extent to which the specific measure focus is evidence-based, important to making significant gains in healthcare quality, and improving health outcomes for a specific high-priority (high-impact) aspect of healthcare where there is variation in or overall less-than-optimal performance.

2. Scientific Acceptability of Measure Properties: Extent to which the measure, as specified, produces consistent (reliable) and credible (valid) results about the quality of care when implemented.

3. Feasibility: Extent to which the specifications, including measure logic, required data that are readily available or could be captured without undue burden and can be implemented for performance measurement.

4. Usability and Use: Extent to which potential audiences (e.g., consumers, purchasers, providers, policymakers) are using or could use performance results for both accountability and performance improvement to achieve the goal of high-quality, efficient healthcare for individuals or populations.

5. Comparison to Related or Competing Measures: If a measure meets the above criteria and there are endorsed or new related measures

(either the same measure focus or the same target population) or competing measures (both the same measure focus and the same target population), the measures are compared to address harmonization and/or selection of the best measure.

More information about NQF approved/endorsed measures is found at the Measures, Reports & Tools [bib#185] website including a list and detailed description of all NQF-Endorsed Measures at QPS [bib#186] which is "*NQF's measure search too*l". Each measure is assigned a unique NQF Identifier Number (NQF#).

The Centers for Medicare and Medicaid Services (CMS) also has a Measures Management System (MMS [bib#187]) which is:

"*a standardized system for developing and maintaining the quality measures used in its various initiatives and programs. Measure developers should follow this standardized system which includes a core set of business processes and decision criteria when developing, implementing, and maintaining quality measures*".

Included in MMS is the CMS Quality Measures Inventory [bib#188]:

"*which is a compilation of measures used by CMS in various quality, reporting and payment programs. The Inventory lists each measure by program, reporting measure specifications including, but not limited to, numerator, denominator, exclusion criteria, Meaningful Measures domain, measure type, and National Quality Forum (NQF) endorsement status*".

Each measure is assigned a unique CMS Measure Inventory Tool (CMIT) Identifier Number.

CMS and the Office of the National Coordinator for Health IT (ONC [bib#189]) have developed Electronic Clinical Quality Improvement (eCQI [bib#190]) measures which are intended:

"*to improve care given to patients by measuring how patients are treated and, most importantly, how well those patients do afterward. ... measure the performance of hospitals, clinicians, and others who provide healthcare services. The "e" in eCQMs means that performance is measured using data pulled from an EHR*".

There are two lists of eCQI measures (eCGMs): one for Eligible Hospital/Critical Access Hospital eCQMs [bib#191] and another for Eligible Professional/Eligible Clinician eCQMs [bib#192]. Each eCGM has a unique eCQM Identifier Number.

The measures listed above are not mutually exclusive; the same measure may be in each of the three datasets and have a NQF #, CMIT Identifier Number, and an eCQI Identifier Number. For example, Breast Cancer Screening is:

- NQF2372 [bib#193]
- CMIT5779 [bib#194]
- eCQM CMS125v7 [bib#195]

Although clearly, any healthcare organization can choose any quality measure it wishes, it is often advantageous to use those on one or more of the three lists described above (NQF, CMIT, eCQM). One advantage is that it allows for benchmarking because the measures are used by so many healthcare organizations.

Benchmarking [bib#196] "*is comparing one's processes and performance metrics to the best performance and practices in the industry*". Benchmarking is useful [bib#197] "*to learn where an organization is performing well against its peers, and where it needs improvement. Usually this information is used for identifying opportunities for improvement initiatives and marketing purposes (rankings, etc.)*".

L1 Discussion Question: Relative Quality Importance of the Six Dimensions of Health Care Quality

The quality domains listed as the Six Dimensions of Health Care Quality in *Crossing the Global Quality Chasm: Improving Health Care Worldwide* [bib#84], are:

1. Safety
2. Effectiveness
3. Person-Centeredness
4. Accessibility, Timeliness, Affordability
5. Efficiency
6. Equity.

Although they are listed as dimensions/domains of Health Care Quality, they can also be considered dimensions/domains of Healthcare Organization Quality.

Do you think that they are all equally important to the quality of the healthcare organization? If not, how would you rank order them in terms of importance?

L1 Quiz and "Create Your Own Healthcare Organization Quality Improvement Program"

L1 Quiz

Question 1

The "degree to which health services for individuals and populations increase the likelihood of desired health outcomes and are consistent with current professional knowledge" is a definition of:

A. Health care quality
B. Health care facilities
C. Health care policy
D. Health care reimbursement

The answer to this question is found in Topic 1 and in the Lesson One Quiz Answer Key at the end of the Lesson One Quiz.

Question 2

The "*degree to which the health care delivered by the healthcare organization consistently reflects current professional knowledge/standards while meeting the patient/customer personal health outcome expectations/requirements*" is a definition of:

A. Drug development quality
B. Reimbursement quality
C. Healthcare organization quality
D. Policy quality

The answer to this question is found in Topic 1 and in the Lesson One Quiz Answer Key at the end of the Lesson One Quiz.

Question 3

Quality improvement in healthcare organizations can be defined as the: "*systematic and continuous actions that lead to measurable improvement healthcare organization quality; that is, systematic and continuous actions that lead to measurable improvement in the degree to which the health care delivered by the healthcare organization consistently reflects current professional knowledge/standards while meeting the patient/customer personal health outcome expectations/requirements*".

A. True
B. False

The answer to this question is found in Topic 1 and in the Lesson One Quiz Answer Key at the end of the Lesson One Quiz.

Question 4

At the core of Six Sigma methodology are DMAIC and DMADV. DMAIC stands for:

A. Define, Measure, Appropriate, Improvise, Control

B. Define, Manipulate, Appropriate, Improvise, Control

C. Define, Measure, Analyze, Improve, Control

D. Define, Manipulate, Appropriate, Improve, Combine

The answer to this question is found in Topic 2 and in the Lesson One Quiz Answer Key at the end of the Lesson One Quiz.

Question 5

The basic strategy of Lean Six Sigma is to first use the Lean strategy to eliminate waste to make the processes _____ effective. Once that is accomplished, the Six Sigma strategy is used to reduce errors/defects in the Lean streamlined processes by either improving them or replacing them.

The answer to this question is found in Topic 2 and in the Lesson One Quiz Answer Key at the end of the Lesson One Quiz.

Question 6

The PDSA cycle is part of a quality improvement strategy. PDSA stands for Plan-Do-Study-Act.

A. True

B. False

The answer to this question is found in Topic 2 and in the Lesson One Quiz Answer Key at the end of the Lesson One Quiz.

Question 7

Which of the following is **not** one of the Six Dimensions of Health Care Quality?

A. Efficiency

B. Elevation/Altitude

C. Safety

D. Accessibility, Timeliness, Affordability

The answer to this question is found in Topic 3 and in the Lesson One Quiz Answer Key at the end of the Lesson One Quiz.

Question 8

The domain of effectiveness quality involves ensuring that healthcare organization patients/customers are provided with the optimal care for their situation; that is, they are provided with evidence-based health care which does not underuse appropriate, effective care and does not overuse ineffective, inappropriate care.

A. True
B. False

The answer to this question is found in Topic 3 and in the Lesson One Quiz Answer Key at the end of the Lesson One Quiz.

Question 9

The domain of person-centeredness quality involves ensuring that delivered health care in the healthcare organization is person/patient-centered; that is, each person is treated as an individual and that individual's wishes, preferences, needs, and values are respected and incorporated into health care delivery.

A. True
B. False

The answer to this question is found in Topic 3 and in the Lesson One Quiz Answer Key at the end of the Lesson One Quiz.

Question 10

NIST stands for:

A. National Invitational Standards and Time
B. National Institute of Standards and Technology
C. Numerical Institute of Standards and Time

The answer to this question is found in Topic 4 and in the Lesson One Quiz Answer Key at the end of the Lesson One Quiz.

Question 11
AHRQ stands for:

A. Accurate Health Reimbursement and Quality
B. Agency for Healthcare Research and Quality
C. Agency for Healthcare Rebuilding Quantitative

The answer to this question is found in Topic 4 and in the Lesson One Quiz Answer Key at the end of the Lesson One Quiz.

Question 12
ASQ stands for The American Society for Quality

A. True
B. False

The answer to this question is found in Topic 4 and in the Lesson One Quiz Answer Key at the end of the Lesson One Quiz.

Question 13
Quality measures which are related to the healthcare organization's structure; which describe the healthcare organization itself are called:

A. Process Quality Measures
B. Structural Quality Measures
C. Outcome Quality Measures

The answer to this question is found in Topic 5 and in the Lesson One Quiz Answer Key at the end of the Lesson One Quiz.

Question 14
_____ Quality Measures are those related to the healthcare organization's processes. Such measures describe what happens in the healthcare organization.

The answer to this question is found in Topic 5 and in the Lesson One Quiz Answer Key at the end of the Lesson One Quiz.

Question 15

Outcome Quality Measures are those related to the outcome (effect) of the healthcare organization's structure and process.

A. True
B. False

The answer to this question is found in Topic 5 and in the Lesson One Quiz Answer Key at the end of the Lesson One Quiz.

L1 Quiz Answer Key

Q1 = A; Q2 = C; Q3 = A; Q4 = C; Q5 = cost; Q6 = A; Q7 = B; Q8 = A; Q9 = A; Q10 = B; Q11 = B; Q12 = A; Q13 = B; Q14 = Process; Q15 = A

L1 "Create Your Own Healthcare Organization Quality Improvement Program"

In Lesson Four, you will *Design a Healthcare Organization Quality Improvement Program*. This competency development task requires that you synthesize content to create your own quality improvement program within a healthcare organization the way you would have things run in the best of all worlds. The type of healthcare organization is your choice (e.g., physical therapy office, dentist office, pharmacy, hospital, doctor's office).

Your synthesized information will be organized as an electronic spreadsheet. An example of a completed spreadsheet project is found in *Appendix B: Spreadsheet Example*. The spreadsheet is an artifact which you can circulate to colleagues or use for a talk or presentation event. Many people use Microsoft Excel for this purpose. However, there are many software options other than Excel. Some are available at no cost such as Calc [bib#198] which is part of LibreOffice [bib#199].

Eleven (11) content items and six (6) design items are suggested for the electronic spreadsheet task to develop competency. However, it is best not to wait until Lesson Four to begin to synthesize content to create your own quality improvement program within a healthcare organization. The earlier in your learning path that you begin this creation process, the better your own quality improvement program within a healthcare organization will be.

So in each lesson prior to Lesson Four, there will be an opportunity to begin to synthesize material – an opportunity to begin to create your own quality improvement program within a healthcare organization using material presented in that lesson. Of the eleven (11) suggested content items for the completed spreadsheet, seven (7) are suggested for consideration in this lesson. Each one of the seven is posted below and includes an expanded description as well as an example. They are:

Suggested Spreadsheet Content Item 1

The name of your healthcare organization in which you will design your quality improvement program.

The name should be original and give some sense to healthcare consumers as to the healthcare products found in your organization.

Example: Charles Harbor General Hospital (CHGH)

Suggested Spreadsheet Content Item 2

A brief description of your healthcare organization; what your healthcare organization does.

The description should be a few sentences which concisely and clearly summarize for healthcare consumers the type of healthcare organization, its location, and its products.

Example: Charles Harbor General Hospital (CHGH) is a private, non-profit, general hospital in Massachusetts. It has an emergency room and a full range of clinical specialties (e.g., internal medicine, general surgery, oncology, cardiology, infectious disease, pediatrics).

Suggested Spreadsheet Content Item 3

A brief description of the quality improvement framework/model you use in your healthcare organization and why. You can use one discussed in the book (e.g., Lean, Six Sigma) or choose another.

There is no right or wrong answer to this question. It just has to be reasoned and make sense.

Example: CHGH uses Lean Six Sigma because of the focus on first using the Lean strategy to eliminate waste (make the processes more cost effective) and then using Six Sigma to reduce errors/defects in the Lean streamlined processes by either improving them or replacing them. It makes little sense to focus on process effectiveness before the processes have been streamlined.

Suggested Spreadsheet Content Item 4

A choice and listing of one of the six health care/healthcare organization quality domains on which to focus your quality improvement program. Include a brief description as to why you chose that domain.

The quality domains listed as the Six Dimensions of Health Care Quality, are:

1. *Safety*
2. *Effectiveness*
3. *Person-Centeredness*
4. *Accessibility, Timeliness, Affordability*
5. *Efficiency*
6. *Equity*

Although they are listed as dimensions/domains of Health Care Quality, they can also be considered dimensions/domains of Healthcare Organization Quality. There is no right or wrong answer to this question. It just has to be reasoned and make sense.

Example: CHGH focuses the quality improvement program on person-centeredness. CHGH considers patient/customer satisfaction to be essential to quality at CHGH. A key to patient/customer satisfaction is ensuring that all organizational processes are person-centered.

<u>Suggested Spreadsheet Content Item 5</u>

A brief outline of the key components of your quality improvement program in your chosen quality domain.

HRSA states that all successful Quality Improvement (QI) programs in healthcare organizations include a focus on:

1. *The operation of the healthcare organization as a system and sub-systems comprised of resources/inputs (e.g., health care delivery professionals), activities/processes (e.g., health care delivery actions), and outputs/outcomes (e.g., change in patient/customer health status).*

2. *Patient/customer exceptions/requirements of the healthcare organization as a whole and, specifically, the health care delivered.*

3. *The need for everyone in the healthcare organization to work as a team with a common goal of QI.*

4. *Collecting and analyzing both qualitative and quantitative data to track quality.*

There is no right or wrong answer to this question. It just has to be reasoned and make sense.

Example: CHGH's person-centeredness quality improvement program is aimed at continuously improving the quality of person-centeredness in all aspects of CHGH functioning. To that purpose the quality improvement program is coordinated by the Office of Quality Improvement which actively:

- Views CHGH as a system within which is a sub-system of processes related to ensuring person-centeredness quality. The person-centeredness quality system cuts across all departments and units at CHGH.

- Understands and respects the CHGH patient/customer expectations/requirements of person-centeredness quality when interacting with CHGH.

- Ensures that all CHGH personnel work as a team to improve person-centeredness quality.

- Collects and analyzes both qualitative and quantitative data to track person-centeredness quality across all of CHGH.

Suggested Spreadsheet Content Item 6

A list of one or more quality improvement professional organizations to which you would belong. It could be one listed in the lesson or another one. Include a brief description of your reasoning for the choice.

There is no right or wrong answer to this question. It just has to be reasoned and make sense.

Example: American Society for Quality (ASQ) because of the large array of quality resources available to members.

Suggested Spreadsheet Content Item 7

A brief description of which of the three types of measures (structural, procedural, or outcome) is/are the focus of your quality improvement program and why.

There is no right or wrong answer to this question. It just has to be reasoned and make sense.

Example: Outcome measures are the focus. For person-centeredness quality, the outcome, the perception of person-centeredness by patients/customers is the key measure. It matters little how hard CHGH tries – what the structure and process are – if the person-centeredness outcome/value from the perspective of the patient/customer is not of high quality.

L1 Trivia Question and Virtual Field Trip

L1 Trivia Question

Almost everyone loves a trivia question – a question about a little known, but interesting, fun fact. Each lesson has one trivia question. The answer is in the Lesson One Trivia Question Answer section.

Question:

Public Law 104-191, the Health Insurance Portability and Accountability Act (HIPAA) of 1996, protects the privacy of patient health information. A different federal law protects the privacy of student education records. *What is the "common" name of the law that protects student information?*

L1 Trivia Question Answer

The answer to the Lesson One trivia question is:

The Family Educational Rights and Privacy Act (FERPA)

For more information, please see:

- U.S. Department of Education, Family Educational Rights and Privacy Act (FERPA) [bib#200]

- Wikipedia, Family Educational Rights and Privacy Act [bib#201]

The oldest continually operating educational institution in the United States is Boston Latin School [bib#202]. It was founded on April 23, 1635 by the Town of Boston. The first classes were held in a private home. Five of the 56 signers of the Declaration of Independence had attended BLS: Samuel Adams, Benjamin Franklin, John Hancock, William Hooper, and Robert Treat Paine. Today Boston Latin School (BLS) is a Boston public school for grades 7 through 12.

L1 Virtual Field Trip

Everyone loves a road trip/field trip so each lesson includes a "*virtual field trip*" to the often hidden places of interest on the web.

Lesson One's virtual field trip is to the National Gallery of Art [bib#203] in Washington, DC.

"The National Gallery of Art was conceived and given to the people of the United States by Andrew W. Mellon (1855–1937). Mellon was a financier and art collector from Pittsburgh who came to Washington in 1921 to serve as secretary of the treasury. During his years of public service he came to believe that the United States should have a national art museum equal to those of other great nations.

In 1936 Mellon wrote to President Franklin D. Roosevelt offering to donate his superb art collection for a new museum and to use his own funds to construct a building for its use. With the president's support, Congress accepted Mellon's gift, which included a sizable endowment, and established the National Gallery of Art in March 1937. Construction began that year at a site on the National Mall along Constitution Avenue between Fourth and Seventh Street NW, near the foot of Capitol Hill."

The quality of the holdings at the National Gallery of Art is exceptional. But as the video for Lesson One shows, quality and quality improvement are frequently in the details. The video shows the work of a mount maker – the person who makes the mounts on which museum holdings sit or hang. The quality of a mount is judged by both its sturdiness and its "*invisibility*" – it should not take away from the object it displays.

*****

Video [bib#204]*: The video for the Lesson One Virtual Field Trip – **The Mount Maker** – is a YouTube video produced by the National Gallery of Art. It shows the work of a mount maker meticulously creating small brass fittings by hand. The link for the video is:*
https://www.youtube.com/watch?v=ORIs2HiwHzg

*****

Lesson Two (L2): Quality and Quality Improvement Measures in Healthcare Organizations

L2 Competency Objective

This lesson provides an overview of quality and quality improvement measures in healthcare organizations. The competency objective is:

- Define quality and quality improvement measures in healthcare organizations.

L2 Content and Discussion

This lesson provides an overview of quality and quality improvement measures in healthcare organizations. Upon successful completion of this lesson, you will be able to: define quality and quality improvement measures in healthcare organizations. There are topic questions, a discussion question, a quiz, a trivia question, and a field trip. The lesson should take 4 - 6 hours of work to successfully complete. There are also videos which provide supplemental content which can help you better define your personal learning path. There are many wonderful videos in the public domain which are relevant to the topics in this book.

This lesson addresses five (5) topics organized as questions. An answer for the healthcare organization quality improvement program you are proposing is provided for each question. The purpose of the answer is to help you organize your thinking and come to your own conclusions and answer consistent with your personal learning goal. The questions/topics for Lesson Two are:

1. What are the medical quality measures in healthcare organizations?

2. What are the dental quality measures in healthcare organizations?

3. What are the pharmacy quality measures in healthcare organizations?

4. What are the health (medical, dental, prescription drug) insurance plan quality measures?

5. What are the public health quality measures established by healthcare organizations?

L2 Topic 1 (T1). What are the medical quality measures in healthcare organizations?

Some of the specific measures used in medical healthcare organizations (e.g., hospitals, physician offices) were discussed in Lesson One. These include:

- National Quality Forum (NQF), NQF-Endorsed Measures (QPS [bib#186]); each with a unique NQF Identifier Number (NQF#)

- The Centers for Medicare and Medicaid Services (CMS), Measures Management System (MMS [bib#187]) measures listed in the CMS Quality Measures Inventory [bib#188]; each with a unique CMS Measure Inventory Tool (CMIT) Identifier Number

- CMS and the Office of the National Coordinator for Health IT (ONC [bib#189]), Electronic Clinical Quality Improvement (eCQI[bib#190]) measures (eCGMs); each with a unique eCQM Identifier Number

Although each of these measures and any other can be used by any medical healthcare organization for internal purposes and improvement, some measures are required or strongly encouraged for use and reporting to external organizations (e.g., reimbursement organizations, ranking organizations).

This section addresses:

- Medical Quality Measures Linked to Reimbursement
- Medical Quality Measures Not Linked to Reimbursement

L2-T1. Medical Quality Measures Linked to Reimbursement

Medicaid payments (reimbursement) to states require the reporting of quality measures. In order for a state to receive Medicaid funds [bib#205] the state:

> "*must meet numerous requirements regarding the proper and efficient administration of their Medicaid programs ... a managed care quality assessment and improvement strategy (i.e., a state quality strategy) ... an annual external independent review of the quality*".

The parameters of this quality requirement are discussed at the Medicaid.gov, Quality of Care [bib#206] website. Listed on this website are quality measures for which data should be collected by the state and reported. These include, but are not limited to:

- Child Core Set [bib#207] related to the Medicaid Quality Improvement Initiatives [bib#208]

- Adult Core Set [bib#209] and Nationwide Adult Consumer Assessment of Healthcare Providers and Systems (CAHPS [bib#210]) related to the Medicaid Quality Improvement Initiatives [bib#208]

The Medicaid quality improvement initiatives – and the relationship of quality measures to reimbursement – are part of the overall National Quality Strategy (NQS [bib#211]) which is coordinated by the Agency for Healthcare Research and Quality (AHRQ) on behalf of the U.S. Department of Health and Human Services (HHS).

Most healthcare organizations receive reimbursement (payment) from private (commercial) and public (government) third-party payers. These payers generally require healthcare organizations to demonstrate that the quality of the health care is worth the reimbursement and, thus, tie reimbursement to quality either directly or generally.

To meet the common quality reporting needs of payer organizations and to ease the administration reporting burden on healthcare organizations, The Core Quality Measures Collaborative [bib#212] (a.k.a., The Collaborative or CQMC) was formed in 2014. It is:

"led by the America's Health Insurance Plans (AHIP) and its member plans' Chief Medical Officers, leaders from CMS and the National Quality Forum (NQF), as well as national physician organizations, employers and consumers".

The Core Quality Measures are organized as eight core measure sets. They are:

1. Accountable Care Organizations (ACOs), Patient Centered Medical Homes (PCMH), and Primary Care [bib#213]
2. Cardiology [bib#214]
3. Gastroenterology [bib#215]
4. HIV and Hepatitis C [bib#216]
5. Medical Oncology [bib#217]
6. Obstetrics and Gynecology [bib#218]
7. Orthopedics [bib#219]
8. Pediatrics [bib#220]

Some of the measures in the above core measure sets are from the Healthcare Effectiveness Data and Information Set (HEDIS [bib#154]). HEDIS data is collected by the National Committee for Quality Assurance (NCQA) from health insurance plans, healthcare organizations, and government agencies. HEDIS contains more than 90 measures organized into six health care domains. The domains are:

1. Effectiveness of Care
2. Access/Availability of Care
3. Experience of Care
4. Utilization and Risk Adjusted Utilization
5. Health Plan Descriptive Information
6. Measures Collected Using Electronic Clinical Data Systems

Some of the other measures in the above core measure sets are from surveys developed for the Consumer Assessment of Healthcare Providers and Systems (CAHPS) program [bib#221] operated by the Agency for Healthcare Research and Quality (AHRQ) whose purpose is the:

"*development and widespread use of a variety of standardized patient surveys that enable health care providers, purchasers, and regulators to track, compare, and improve patients' experiences in different health care settings*".

The CAHPS surveys [bib#222]:

"ask patients to report on their experiences with a range of health care services at multiple levels of the delivery system. Some CAHPS surveys ask about patients' experiences with providers, such as medical, groups, practice sites, and surgical centers, or with care for specific health conditions. Other surveys ask enrollees about their experiences with health plans and related programs. Finally, several surveys ask about experiences with care delivered in facilities, including hospitals, dialysis centers, and nursing homes".

One of the most widely-known CAHPS surveys is the Adult Hospital Survey (HCAHPS [bib#223]) which "*asks people 18 and older about their experiences with medical, surgical, or obstetric care provided in an inpatient setting*". HCAHPS is implemented by [bib#224] The Centers for Medicare & Medicaid Services (CMS); more than 4000 hospitals in the United States administer the HCAHPS as part of their quality improvement programs.

CMS is using some of the Core Quality Measures for Medicare reimbursement via the Quality Payment Program (QPP [bib#225]). The QPP was created and required via the Medicare Access and CHIP Reauthorization Act of 2015 (MACRA [bib#226]) which stipulated that healthcare organizations receiving Medicare reimbursement had to participate in one of the following payment (reimbursement) programs:

- Advanced Alternative Payment models (APMs)
- The Merit-based Incentive Payment System (MIPS)

The Advanced Alternative Payment Models (APMs [bib#227]) program provides an incentive payment "*to provide high-quality and cost-efficient care. APMs can apply to a specific clinical condition, a care episode, or a population.*" To participate in the CMS APM reimbursement program, the healthcare organization must participate in a CMS-approved APM; each has its own quality data requirement. Some of the CMS-approved APMs are:

- Bundled Payments for Care Improvement Advanced Model (BPCI Advanced) [bib#228]

- Medicare Accountable Care Organization (ACO) Track 1+ Model [bib#229]

- Next Generation ACO Model [bib#230]

- Oncology Care Model (OCM) - Two-Sided Risk [bib#231]

- Comprehensive Care for Joint Replacement (CJR) Payment Model (Track 1- CEHRT) [bib#232]

Advanced APM participants are also subject to the MIPS reporting and payment adjustment requirements if they do not meet QPP-specified thresholds.

The Merit-based Incentive Payment System (MIPS [bib#233]) assigns a score from 0 to 100 to each participant based on the value (data) submitted to CMS for measures in four categories:

- Quality [bib#234] (45 percent of the final score in 2019); participants must choose six measures on which to submit data from a list of almost 300 measures.

- Promoting Interoperability [bib#235] (25 percent of the final score in 2019); participants must first select a measure set on which to submit data based on the Certified EHR Technology (CEHRT) in use; participants then select a subset of the measures in that set on which to submit data; the two measure set choices are: 1) Promoting Interoperability Objectives and Measures, or 2) Promoting Interoperability Transition Objectives and Measures.

- Improvement Activities [bib#236] (15 percent of the final score in 2019); participants must choose a subset of measures on which to submit data from a list of more than 100 measures; there are three subsets from which measures can be chosen: 1) two high-weighted activities, 2) one high-weighted activity and two medium-weighted activities; or 3) at least four medium-weighted activities.

- Cost [bib#237] (15 percent of the final score in 2019); participants do not submit data for the cost measures; CMS obtains the required data automatically through administrative claims data.

Those participants with a very high score have the standard payment/reimbursement increased (receive an incentive payment). Those with a very low score have the standard payment/reimbursement reduced.

*****

> *Video* [bib#238]*: The video for Topic 1 – **What is the Scoring Methodology for the Merit-based Incentive Payment System?** – is a YouTube video produced CMSHHSgov. This video discusses how points are awarded, how the Final Score is calculated, and how payment adjustments are made in the Merit-based Incentive Payment System (MIPS). The link for the video is:*
> https://www.youtube.com/watch?v=OHOEQRo4qOs

*****

L2-T1. Medical Quality Measures Not Linked to Reimbursement

There are also many structured and not-structured healthcare organization quality measures not used for reimbursement. Many of these are directed toward patients/consumers to aid in their evaluation of which healthcare organizations to use for health care delivery products and services. Some are required for accreditation or certification.

One example are the quality measures incorporated into Joint Commission programs [bib#239] discussed in detail on the Joint Commission Performance Measurement [bib#240] website and Accountability Measures [bib#241] website.

The Leapfrog Group [bib#242] "*is a national nonprofit organization driving a movement for giant leaps forward in the quality and safety of American health care*". Healthcare organizations can voluntarily participate in one of the Leapfrog surveys. The flagship survey is the Hospital Survey [bib#243]. Using survey data, the Leapfrog Group rates the overall quality of the healthcare organization. Consumers can compare hospitals at the Leapfrog Choosing the right hospital [bib#244] website. The most highly rated hospitals are found on the Top Hospitals [bib#245] website.

The comparison of hospital quality is also the goal of the Medicare.gov Hospital Compare [bib#246] website. The measures used for Hospital Compare are discussed on the Measures and current data collection periods [bib#247] website. Based on these measures, each hospital is assigned a Hospital Compare overall hospital rating [bib#248] from one star (lowest) to five stars (highest).

Other structured quality ratings/rankings of healthcare organizations include, but are not limited to, U.S. News Health Care Rankings [bib#249], and U.S. News Nursing Home Rankings [bib#250]. Consumers also provide non-structured quality ratings for healthcare organizations through websites and services such as:

- Yelp (Health) [bib#251]
- RateMDs [bib#252]
- Healthgrades [bib#253]
- Vitals [bib#254]

There is also a fairly large amount of publicly available data on healthcare organization quality and other measures which anyone can access. Such data can be used for a variety of medical healthcare organization quality-related activities (e.g., research, constructing a new quality measure). Good sources of such data include, but are not limited to:

- DATA.GOV [bib#255] especially HealthData.gov [bib#256]
- Health IT Dashboard, Data [bib#257]
- Centers for Disease Control and Prevention (CDC), Data Access, Public-Use Data Files and Documentation [bib#258]
- openFDA, Datasets [bib#259]
- Data.Medicare.gov [bib#260]

L2 Topic 2 (T2). What are the dental quality measures in healthcare organizations?

As with medical healthcare organizations, dental healthcare organizations can use any quality measure of their choosing for internal purposes and improvement. Unlike medical healthcare organizations, however, dental organizations have very few measures, by comparison to medical healthcare organizations, which are required or strongly encouraged for use and reporting to external organizations (e.g., reimbursement organizations, ranking organizations).

This section addresses:

- Dental Quality Measures Linked to Reimbursement
- Dental Quality Measures Not Linked to Reimbursement

L2-T2. Dental Quality Measures Linked to Reimbursement

As stated in Topic 1, in order for a state to receive Medicaid funds [bib#205] (to receive Medicaid payments/reimbursement) states must report quality measures. The parameters of this quality requirement are discussed at the Medicaid.gov, Quality of Care [bib#206] website.. Listed on this website are quality measures for which data should be collected by the state and reported. Some of the quality measures address dental care and oral health. Specifically, they are two measures in the Child Core Set [bib#207] related to the Oral Health Quality Improvement Initiative [bib#261]:

- Dental and Oral Health Services: Dental Sealants for 6–9 Year-Old Children at Elevated Caries Risk (SEAL-CH)

- Dental and Oral Health Services: Percentage of Eligibles Who Received Preventive Dental Services (PDENT-CH)

The American Dental Association (ADA) Dental Quality Alliance (DQA [bib#262]) suggests the use of additional measures including some from the National Quality Forum (NQF), NQF-Endorsed Measures (QPS [bib#186]) such as:

- NQF2511 [bib#263]: Percentage of enrolled children under age 21 years who received at least one dental service within the reporting year (Utilization of Services, Dental Services)

- NQF2528 [bib#264]: Percentage of enrolled children aged 1-21 years who are at "elevated" risk (i.e., "moderate" or "high") who received at least 2 topical fluoride applications within the reporting year (Prevention: Topical Fluoride for Children at Elevated Caries Risk, Dental Services)

Some dental healthcare organizations receive reimbursement (payment) from private (commercial) and government (public) third-party payers. These payers generally require healthcare organizations to demonstrate that the quality of the health care is worth the reimbursement and, thus, tie reimbursement to quality either directly or generally.

Such quality demonstration for dental healthcare organizations may involve measures from the Dental Plan Survey [bib#265] offered by the Consumer Assessment of Healthcare Providers and Systems (CAHPS) program [bib#221] operated by the Agency for Healthcare Research and Quality (AHRQ).   Although many of the measures on the CAHPS Dental Plan Survey ask patients/customers about their experience with the dental insurance plan, some measures address:

- Care from Dentists and Staff
- Overall Rating of the Dentist
- Overall Rating of Dental Care

The Dental Plan Survey was developed by [bib#266] the American Institutes for Research (AIR [bib#267]) and TRICARE [bib#268] which is the Department of Defense's "*health care program for uniformed service members, retirees, and their families around the world*" and then made available to the CAHPS program.

*****

> ***Video*** [bib#269]: *The video for Topic 2 – **Your Inner Fish:**
> **The Evolution of your Teeth** – is a YouTube video produced
> by PBS. This video discusses the history and evolution of
> human teeth. The link for the video is:*
> https://www.youtube.com/watch?v=ohq3CoOKEoo

*****

L2-T2. Dental Quality Measures Not Linked to Reimbursement

The American Dental Association (ADA) Dental Quality Alliance (DQA) is also working on voluntary dental Practice Assessments [bib#270] quality measures to: "*assist practices in getting started with measuring towards quality improvement*". Updates on this project are found at the DQA Measure Activities [bib#271] website.

However, most dental healthcare organization quality measures which are not directly linked to reimbursement are directed toward patients/consumers and are often developed/reported by patients/consumers. These include:

- Yelp [bib#272]
- RateMDs, Dentist [bib#273]
- Healthgrades, Find a Dentist [bib#274]
- Healthgrades, Find an Orthodontics Specialist [bib#275]
- Vitals, Find a Dentist Near Me [bib#276]
- RankMyDentist [bib#277]

There is also a fairly large amount of publicly available data on dental healthcare organization quality and other measures which anyone can access. Such data can be used for a variety of dental healthcare organization quality-related activities (e.g., research, constructing a new quality measure). Good sources of such data include, but are not limited to:

- American Dental Association (ADA), Health Policy Institute, Data Center [bib#278]

- DATA.GOV [bib#255] especially HealthData.gov [bib#256]

- Centers for Disease Control and Prevention (CDC), Data Access, Public-Use Data Files and Documentation [bib#258] especially Oral Health Data [bib#279]

  Additional interesting resources are:

- How to Find a Good Dentist [bib#280]

- Measuring the Quality of Care [bib#281]: The Importance of Dentist Involvement in Determining Quality Measures

- Measuring Up [bib#282]: Implementing a Dental Quality Measure in the Electronic Health Record Context

- Clinical Performance Measures and Quality Improvement System Considerations for Dental Education [bib#283]

- Healthy People 2020: Oral Health [bib#284]

L2 Topic 3 (T3). What are the pharmacy quality measures in healthcare organizations?

There are two major aspects of pharmacy quality. One is the quality of the pharmacy and the other is the quality of the pharmaceuticals (medications) dispensed by the pharmacy. Clearly, the quality of all medical equipment and devices used in any healthcare organization or sold/rented by any healthcare organization is also an issue, but pharmaceuticals are so central to today's health care delivery that they deserve special discussion.

This section discusses:

- Pharmacy Quality Measures

- Pharmaceutical Quality Measures

L2-T3. Pharmacy Quality Measures

Reimbursement/payment for a pharmacy is usually directly linked to the pharmaceuticals dispensed. Each pharmaceutical (medication) has a price and the pricing of that pharmaceutical is usually established elsewhere. As such, no specific pharmacy quality measures affect that drug product price and how much the pharmacy is reimbursed/paid for that medication product.

In addition, the medication product is usually one which has been mass produced outside of the pharmacy. The pharmacy responsibility is primarily to ensure that the prescribed mass produced medication is delivered correctly (as prescribed) to the correct person. Any individual pharmacy and pharmacist only produces the medication if they are compounding; such pharmacies/pharmacists are called a compounding pharmacy/pharmacist. The Professional Compounding Centers of America (PCCA) defines compounding [bib#285] as:

> "*the art and science of creating personalized medicine. It all starts with a problem: the child who can't swallow pills, the patient with a gluten allergy, the much-needed drug that's in short supply. For whatever reason, many people aren't served by mass-produced medications.*
>
> *That's where compounding comes in. Special flavorings, unique dosage forms, innovative delivery methods – using these tools and more, compounding pharmacists work with prescribers to fill a gap in health care through customized solutions for specific patient needs.*"

Before mass produced medications, all pharmacies were, at least in part, compounding pharmacies [bib#286]: "*Pharmacists continued to compound most prescriptions until the early 1950s when the majority of dispensed drugs came directly from the large pharmaceutical companies.*"

Merck [bib#287] is generally considered to be the first industrial pharmaceutical company (first to mass produce medications). Merck began as a single pharmacy (Angel Pharmacy) in Darmstadt, Germany in 1654. This pharmacy transformed over time and in 1827, under the ownership of Heinrich Emanuel Merck, began the mass production manufacturing and selling of alkaloids [bib#288].

The first industrial pharmaceutical company in the United States is generally considered to be Pfizer [bib#289] which began when Charles Pfizer [bib#290] (a chemist) and his cousin, Charles F. Erhart [bib#291] (a candy maker), combined their skills in 1849 in Brooklyn, New York to mass produce and sell almond-toffee flavored santonin [bib#292] – an antiparasitic used to treat intestinal worms.

Many of the "*quality measures*" associated with pharmacies are, in fact, local, state, and federal laws/regulations regarding the operation of a pharmacy. However, there are some quality measures developed specifically for pharmacies such as those developed by pharmacy accreditation associations.

For example, the Center for Pharmacy Practice Accreditation (CPPA [bib#293]) seeks to ensure that those pharmacies with CPPA accreditation provide the "*highest quality care*". Therefore, each of the accreditation programs – Community Pharmacy Practice Accreditation [bib#294], Specialty Pharmacy Practice Accreditation [bib#295], and Telehealth Pharmacy Practice Accreditation [bib#296] – includes a requirement that the pharmacy operate a continuous quality improvement (CQI) program.

Another example is the Accreditation Commission for Health Care (ACHC [bib#297]) which offers Pharmacy Accreditation [bib#298] which requires, in part, that pharmacies "*demonstrate their commitment to providing the highest-quality service through compliance with national regulations and industry best practices*".

ACHC also offers Compounding Pharmacy Accreditation [bib#299] in cooperation with the Pharmacy Compounding Accreditation Board (PCAB). A requirement of the accreditation is the "*pharmacy's commitment to continuous compliance significantly reduces the risk associated with compounding medications and demonstrates a commitment to meeting the highest industry standards for quality and safety*".

Other structured quality ratings/rankings of pharmacy healthcare organizations include, but are not limited to the J.D. Power Healthcare Ratings [bib#300] for:

- Chain Drug Store Pharmacy [bib#301] (Brick and Mortar)
- Mass Merchandisers Pharmacy [bib#302] (Brick and Mortar)
- Supermarket Pharmacy [bib#303] (Brick and Mortar)
- Mail Order Pharmacy [bib#304]

Consumers also provide non-structured quality ratings for pharmacy healthcare organizations through websites and services such as:

- Yelp [bib#272]
- Healthgrades, Find a Pharmacist [bib#305]
- Vitals [bib#254]
- RateMyPharmacy [bib#306]

There is also a fairly large amount of publicly available data on pharmacy healthcare organization quality and other measures which anyone can access. Such data can be used for a variety of pharmacy healthcare organization quality-related activities (e.g., research, constructing a new quality measure). Good sources of such data include, but are not limited to:

- DATA.GOV [bib#255] especially HealthData.gov [bib#256]
- Centers for Disease Control and Prevention (CDC), Data Access, Public-Use Data Files and Documentation [bib#258]
- Data.Medicare.gov [bib#260]

L2-T3. Pharmaceutical Quality Measures

Pharmacy quality and quality improvement are essentially meaningless if the quality of the pharmaceuticals dispensed is poor. And the quality of the pharmaceuticals (medications) is largely out of the control of the individual pharmacy (except for compounding pharmaceuticals). The mass produced pharmaceuticals/medications dispensed by pharmacies have quality controlled external to the pharmacy.

Such quality control is largely the responsibility of the FDA [bib#148] whose "*modern regulatory functions began with the passage of the 1906 Pure Food and Drugs Act*" when it was known as the Bureau of Chemistry within the United States Department of Agriculture (USDA) [bib#307]. It became known as the Food and Drug Administration (FDA) in 1930 and is now part of the United States Department of Health and Human Services (HHS). Many products fall under FDA quality control (safeguard) jurisdiction including drugs [bib#308] dispensed in pharmacies.

FDA approval is needed for drugs to legally enter the United States marketplace. Such approval constitutes the final steps of the Drug Development Process [bib#309] which has five steps:

1. Discovery and Development [bib#310]
2. Preclinical Research [bib#311]
3. Clinical Research [bib#312]
4. FDA Drug Review [bib#313]
5. FDA Post-Market Drug Safety Monitoring [bib#314]

Part of the regulatory process usually includes reviewing data from drug clinical trials [bib#315] (Step 3) and monitoring post-market drug performance (Step 5) via the FDA Adverse Event Reporting System (FAERS) [bib#316] surveillance system and MedWatch: The FDA Safety Information and Adverse Event Reporting Program [bib#317].

A comprehensive list of drugs approved by the FDA can be found at Drugs@FDA: FDA Approved Drug Products [bib#318] website as well as the Orange Book [bib#319]. Downloadable files as well as additional information about these resources can be found at the FDA Resources for Information on Approved Drugs [bib#320] website.

*****

> **Video** [bib#321]*: The video for Topic 3 – **The Drug Discovery Process** –is a YouTube video produced by PhRMAPress. This video provides an overview of the drug discovery process. The link for the video is:*
> https://www.youtube.com/watch?v=DhxD6sVQEYc

*****

Usually pharmacies can only legally dispense drugs which have successfully completed Step 4. However, under right-to-try laws [bib#322] clinicians can prescribe and pharmacies can legally dispense some medications in Step 3. The purpose of right-to-try laws is to allow terminally ill patients to legally try treatments using non-FDA approved devices, drugs, and biologics. The federal Right-to-Try Act [bib#323] was signed into law on May 30, 2018.

It should be noted that compounded drugs are not FDA approved [bib#324]:

> "*Quality requirements for compounded drugs differ depending on the setting where compounding occurs. Drugs compounded in outsourcing facilities are subject to current good manufacturing practice (CGMP) requirements.*
>
> *By contrast, drugs compounded by a licensed pharmacist in a state-licensed pharmacy, or federal facility, or by a physician, in accordance with the conditions of section 503A of the FD&C Act, are exempt from compliance with CGMP requirements. These facilities may be subject to less stringent quality standards set in state law or policy. Such standards may differ state to state.*
>
> *However, regardless of where compounding occurs, whether in a pharmacy, outsourcing facility, or physician's office, other federal requirements apply, including the requirement that drugs not be prepared, packed, or held under unnsanitary conditions.*"

In addition to the FDA Adverse Event Reporting System (FAERS) [bib#316] surveillance system and MedWatch: The FDA Safety Information and Adverse Event Reporting Program [bib#317], consumers also provide non-structured quality ratings for pharmaceuticals through websites and services such as:

- WebMD Drugs and Medications [bib#325]
- DrugRatingz.com [bib#326]
- Ask a Patient [bib#327]
- Iodine.com [bib#328]

There is also a fairly large amount of publicly available data on pharmaceutical quality and other measures which anyone can access. Such data can be used for a variety of pharmaceutical quality-related activities (e.g., research, constructing a new quality measure). Good sources of such data include, but are not limited to:

- DATA.GOV [bib#255] especially HealthData.gov [bib#256]
- openFDA, Datasets [bib#259]

L2 Topic 4 (T4). What are the health (medical, dental, prescription drug) insurance plan quality measures?

Quality measures are not just defined for healthcare organizations which delivery health care. Quality measures are also defined for those healthcare organizations which provide health insurance plans (medical, dental, prescription drug).

This section addresses:

- Medical/Health Insurance Plan Quality Measures
- Dental Insurance Plan Quality Measures
- Prescription Drug Insurance Plan Quality Measures

L2-T4. Medical/Health Insurance Plan Quality Measures

One of the best known quality ratings of medical/health plans is the National Committee for Quality Assurance (NCQA) Health Insurance Plan Ratings [bib#329] for commercial (private, Medicaid, and Medicare) insurance plans. Each rated plan is assigned an overall quality rating from 0 to 5 (five is highest) as well as a 0 to 5 quality rating in each of three categories: Consumer Satisfaction, Prevention, and Treatment. The detailed methodology for calculating each of the quality measures is found at the Methodology [bib#330] website. Each rating uses measures and data from the plan's HEDIS, CAHPS, and NCQA Accreditation.

HEDIS [bib#154] (Healthcare Effectiveness Data and Information Set) data is collected by NCQA. HEDIS contains more than 90 measures organized into six health care domains. The domains are:

1. Effectiveness of Care
2. Access/Availability of Care
3. Experience of Care
4. Utilization and Risk Adjusted Utilization
5. Health Plan Descriptive Information
6. Measures Collected Using Electronic Clinical Data Systems

Consumer Assessment of Healthcare Providers and System surveys (CAHPS surveys [bib#222]) "*ask patients to report on their experiences with a range of health care services at multiple levels of the delivery system ... Some ... surveys ask enrollees about their experiences with health plans and related programs*".

NCQA also includes quality measures in its Health Plan Accreditation (HPA [bib#331]) which seeks to ensure that health plans "*support care that keeps members at optimum levels of health while also controlling costs and meeting government and purchaser requirements*".

Other organizations which accredit health plans also have quality measures such as URAC's Health Plan Accreditation [bib#332] which is an "*assurance that the organization meets rigorous standards and measures of* quality and operational integrity ... Achievement of URAC accreditation demonstrates an organization's clear commitment to quality and continuous improvement."

Medicare also provides Plan Quality and Performance Ratings [bib#333] from 1 to 5 (5 is the highest). The Health Plan Quality Summary Rating [bib#334] gives information about the health plan's quality and performance and includes:

- *"Staying healthy: screening tests and vaccines: Whether members got various screening tests, vaccines, and other check-ups to help them stay healthy.*

- *Managing chronic (long-term) conditions: How often members with certain conditions got recommended tests and treatments to help manage their conditions.*

- *Member experience with the health plan: Member ratings of the plan.*

- *Member complaints and changes in the health plan's performance: How often members had problems with the plan. Includes how much the plan's performance improved (if at all) over time.*

- *Health plan customer service: How well the plan handles member calls and questions."*

*****

> ***Video*** [bib#335]*: The video for Topic 4 – **CMS Star Ratings** – is a YouTube video produced by the American Cancer Society (ACS). This video discusses the Centers for Medicare and Medicaid Services (CMS) Star Ratings, their importance, and how they are calculated. The link for the video is:* https://www.youtube.com/watch?v=fYnts1OOQsA

*****

Healthcare.gov [bib#256], the federal health insurance exchange website, is currently introducing quality ratings [bib#336] for health insurance plans based on *"member experience, medical care, and health plan administration"*.

In addition, J.D. Power Healthcare Ratings [bib#300] are available for:

- Medicare Advantage Plans [bib#337]
- Vision Care Plans [bib#338]

L2-T4. Dental Insurance Plan Quality Measures

The American Dental Association (ADA) Dental Quality Alliance (DQA) has developed a set of quality measures for Medicaid and Dental Plan Assessments [bib#339]. The measures are divided into three categories:

1. Evaluating Utilization (Example: Preventive Services for Children at Elevated Caries Risk: Percentage of all enrolled children who are at *"elevated"* risk (i.e., *"moderate"* or *"high"*) who received a topical fluoride application and/or sealants within the reporting year)

2. Evaluating Quality of Care (Example: Ongoing Care in Adults with Periodontitis: Percentage of enrolled adults aged 30 years and older with a history of periodontitis who received an oral prophylaxis OR scaling/root planing OR periodontal maintenance visit at least 2 times within the reporting year)

3. Evaluating Cost (Example: Per Member Per Month Cost of Clinical Services: Total amount that is paid on direct provision of care (reimbursed for clinical services) per member per month for all enrolled children during the reporting year)

Dental insurance plan accreditation also includes quality measures such as those included in the URAC Dental Plan Accreditation [bib#340] program: *"Dental plans that achieve the URAC Accreditation Seal differentiate themselves by demonstrating a commitment to continuous quality improvement and by verifying their adherence to a set of rigorous quality standards*". In addition, J.D. Power Healthcare Ratings [bib#300] are available for Health Plan Dental Care Satisfaction [bib#341].

L2-T4. Prescription Drug Insurance Plan Quality Measures

In addition to the Health Plan Summary Rating, Medicare also provides Plan Quality and Performance Ratings [bib#333] from 1 to 5 (5 is the highest) for prescription drug plans. The Prescription Drug Plan Quality [bib#342] summary rating gives information about the prescription drug plan's quality and performance and includes:

- "*Drug plan customer service: How well the plan handles member calls and questions.*

- *Member complaints and changes in the drug plan's performance: How often members had problems with the plan. Includes how much the plan's performance improved (if at all) over time.*

- *Member experience with the drug plan: Member ratings of the plan.*

- *Drug safety and accuracy of drug pricing: How accurate the plan's pricing information is and how often members with certain medical conditions are prescribed drugs in a way that is considered safer and clinically recommended for their condition.*"

Individual prescription drug plans are not accredited, but the Pharmacy Benefit Managers (PBMs) [bib#343] who administer the prescription drug plan can be. The Pharmaceutical Care Management Association (PCMA [bib#344]), the national association for PBM**s,** states that:

"PBMs administer prescription drug plans for more than 266 million Americans who have health insurance from a variety of sponsors including: commercial health plans, self-insured employer plans, union plans, Medicare Part D plans, the Federal Employees Health

Benefits Program (FEHBP), state government employee plans, managed Medicaid plans, and others."

The first PBM was founded in 1968 as the Pharmaceutical Card System (PCS). The largest PBM today is Express Scripts [bib#345].

URAC offers Pharmacy Benefit Management Accreditation [bib#346] which requires that the PBM meet "*key benchmarks in service quality*" and "*focus formulary decisions on the safety, efficacy and therapeutic need for drugs first, and focus on cost only after these considerations are met*".

A PBM can also be eligible for the National Committee for Quality Assurance (NCQA) Utilization Management Accreditation [bib#347] which seeks to:

"ensure that patients have the proper care and the required services without overusing resources. NCQA Utilization Management Accreditation helps guarantee that organizations making these decisions are following objective, evidence-based best practices".

CVS Caremark [bib#348], for example, has NCQA [bib#349] Utilization Management Accreditation. CVS Caremark is the PBM [bib#350] for CVS Health.

There is also a fairly large amount of publicly available data on health insurance plan quality and other measures which anyone can access. Such data can be used for a variety of insurance plan quality-related activities (e.g., research, constructing a new quality measure). Good sources of such data include, but are not limited to:

- DATA.GOV [bib#255] especially HealthData.gov [bib#256]
- Census Bureau Health Insurance Datasets [bib#351]
- CMS Health Insurance Exchange Public Use Files (Exchange PUFs) [bib#352]
- Data.Medicare.gov [bib#260]

L2 Topic 5 (T5). What are the public health quality measures established by healthcare organizations?

Some healthcare organizations are involved in population (public) health. The quality measures for such organizations are usually related to the health of the population on which they focus.

- Public Health Quality Initiatives of Healthcare Organizations
- Public Health Quality Measures Used by Healthcare Organizations

L2-T5. Public Health Quality Initiatives of Healthcare Organizations

In the United States, two of the major organizations with a national responsibility for public health quality (responsibility for health quality in the United States as a whole) are the:

1. Surgeon General's Office [bib#353] in association with the Commissioned Corps of the United States Public Health Service (USPHS [bib#354])

2. Centers for Disease Control and Prevention (CDC [bib#355]).

Both are part of [bib#356] the United States Department of Health and Human Services (HHS [bib#357]). Each of these organizations work closely with the local, county, and state Department of Health or Department of Public Health [bib#358] which have public health quality responsibility for that local, county, or state population.

The USPHS began [bib#359] as the U. S. Marine Hospital Service, established by an Act of Congress in 1798, to care for sick and disabled seamen primarily out of concern that seamen were carrying and spreading yellow fever to residents of American port cities. The Marine Hospital Service was reorganized in 1870 and in 1871 the first Supervising Surgeon (now the Surgeon General) was appointed. In 1889, Congress authorized another reorganization which established the Commissioned Corps of the USPHS.

The mission [bib#360] of the USPHS Commissioned Corps is to "*protect, promote, and advance the health and safety of our Nation. As America's uniformed service of public health professionals, the Commissioned Corps achieves its mission through:*

- *Rapid and effective response to public health needs*
- *Leadership and excellence in public health practices*
- *Advancement of public health science*"

The head of the Commission Corps is the Surgeon General who has a focus [bib#361]:

"*on improving the country's health. The Surgeon General communicates the best available scientific information to the public, using the position's platform to reach individuals where they live, work, and play and by issuing scientific documents on critical public health issues ... The Office of the Surgeon General also has its own peer-reviewed journal ... Public Health Reports*" [bib#362].

The Surgeon General's priority public health quality initiatives are:

- Opioids and Addiction [bib#363]
- Tobacco [bib#364]
- Community Health and Economic Prosperity [bib#365]
- Health and National Security [bib#366]
- Oral Health [bib#367]
- Emerging Public Health Threats [bib#368]

*****

Video [bib#369]*: The video for Topic 5 – **Lessons learned**
from the center of America's opioid epidemic – is a YouTube
video produced by TEDMED. This video discusses strategies
to combat the opioid epidemic and improve the quality of
public health. The link for the video is:*
https://www.youtube.com/watch?v=W-CU5Ei9oUU

*****

The CDC began as the Communicable Disease Center [bib#370] in 1942 with one primary mission: to prevent malaria from spreading across the nation. "*Although medical epidemiologists were scarce in those early years, disease surveillance became the cornerstone of CDC's mission of service to the states and over time changed the practice of public health*". CDC 's current mission [bib#371] is:

"*to protect America from health, safety and security threats ...
Whether diseases start at home or abroad, are chronic or acute,
curable or preventable, human error or deliberate attack, CDC fights
disease and supports communities and citizens to do the same.*

*CDC increases the health security of our nation. As the nation's
health protection agency, CDC saves lives and protects people from
health threats. To accomplish our mission, CDC conducts critical
science and provides health information that protects our nation
against expensive and dangerous health threats, and responds when
these arise.*"

CDC supports initiatives which increase the quality of public health. Many of these initiatives are described at the CDC National Health Initiatives, Strategies & Action Plans [bib#372] website. The CDC Strategic Plan [bib#373] states that quality public health *"requires continuous improvement for our most vital assets, which are fundamental to meet our agency's priorities"*.

CDC also sought to improve the quality of local, county, and state health departments with its National Public Health Improvement Initiative

(NPHII [bib#374]) between 2010–2014 which had as one major objective "*improving organizational efficiency and effectiveness through quality improvement activities*".

Currently, the CDC supports "*the implementation of a national voluntary accreditation* [bib#375] *program for state, tribal, local, and territorial health departments*". Accreditation by the Public Health Accreditation Board (PHAB [bib#376]) first became available in 2013. "*The goal of the voluntary national accreditation program is to improve and protect the health of the public by advancing the quality and performance of Tribal, state, local, and territorial public health departments. PHAB's public health department accreditation process seeks to advance quality and performance within public health departments*".

No discussion of public health quality initiatives is complete without mention of the initiative to improve the quality of population health through the elimination of smallpox. The World Health Organization (WHO) led a collaborative effort to eliminate smallpox [bib#377] between 1966 and 1980. Smallpox was officially declared eradicated in 1980; enormously improving the quality of public health across the globe. Just prior to efforts [bib#378] to eradicate the smallpox, an estimated 50 million people contracted smallpox each year. The mortality rate was between 20 percent and 60 percent with most survivors having terrible smallpox scars.

Additional interesting resources about smallpox and the eradication effort can be found at:

- Smallpox: A Great and Terrible Scourge [bib#379]
- Smallpox and Its Eradication [bib#380]
- Global Alert and Response (GAR) – Smallpox [bib#381]
- Control, elimination, eradication and re-emergence of infectious diseases: getting the message right [bib#382]

L2-T5. Public Health Quality Measures Used by Healthcare Organizations

Although the Surgeon General's Office and the USPHS issues reports based [bib#383] on data, it is the CDC which primarily establishes public health quality measures and collects data for national public health quality initiatives. The data collection tools, measures, and some of the collected data are available at the CDC Data and Statistics [bib#384] website. More comprehensive and easily downloadable data for quality and other research are available from the CDC Data Access, Public-Use Data Files and Documentation [bib#385]. Some of the data associated with these measures can be easily accessed from the CDC's Interactive Data Tools and Query Systems [bib#386] website. The CDC also collects and provides Performance Management and Quality Improvement [bib#387] data and benchmarks "*to support state, tribal, local and territorial health departments as they head down the path of improving their performance*".

One national public health quality data collection initiative warrants a special mention: Healthy People [bib#388]. The current Healthy People initiative is Healthy People 2020 (Healthy People 2030 is under development)**.** "*Healthy People provides science-based, 10-year national objectives for improving the health of all Americans*"**.** The goals are [bib#389]:

- "*Attain high-quality, longer lives free of preventable disease, disability, injury, and premature death.*

- *Achieve health equity, eliminate disparities, and improve the health of all groups.*

- *Create social and physical environments that promote good health for all.*

- *Promote quality of life, healthy development, and healthy behaviors across all life stages.*"

Healthy People is organized into more than 40 topic areas and almost 1,200 objectives (measures) on which data is collected and made publicly available at DATA2020 [bib#390]. Twenty-six of the objectives (measures) in 12 topic areas are considered Leading Health Indicators (LHI [bib#391]) "*selected to communicate high-priority health issues and actions that can be taken to address them*".

L2 Discussion Question: Characteristics of a Great Healthcare Organization Quality Measure

There are many ways to measure the quality and quality improvement of healthcare organizations. What do you think are the most important characteristics of any healthcare organization quality measure (e.g., easy to collect, collected by many healthcare organizations so benchmarking is possible)? What do you think are the overall characteristics of a great healthcare organization quality or quality improvement measure?

L2 Quiz and "Create Your Own Healthcare Organization Quality Improvement Program"

L2 Quiz

Question 1

HEDIS data is collected by the National Committee for Quality Assurance (NCQA) from health insurance plans, healthcare organizations, and government agencies. HEDIS stands for _____ Effectiveness Data and Information Set

The answer to this question is found in Topic 1 and in the Lesson Two Quiz Answer Key at the end of the Lesson Two Quiz.

Question 2

The CAHPS program is operated by the Agency for Healthcare Research and Quality (AHRQ) whose purpose is the "*development and widespread use of a variety of standardized patient surveys that enable health care providers, purchasers, and regulators to track, compare, and improve patients' experiences in different health care settings"*. CAHPS stands for:

A. Customer Automated Health Process and Support
B. Consumer Assessment of Healthcare Providers and Systems
C. Customer Acknowledgement of Healthcare Providers and Support
D. Consumer Assessment of Health Process and System

The answer to this question is found in Topic 1 and in the Lesson Two Quiz Answer Key at the end of the Lesson Two Quiz.

Question 3

The Merit-based Incentive Payment System (MIPS) assigns a score from 0 to 100 to each participant based on the value (data) submitted to CMS for measures in four categories. Which of the following is **not** one of the categories?

A. Improvement Activities
B. Quality
C. Staffing
D. Promoting Interoperability

The answer to this question is found in Topic 1 and in the Lesson Two Quiz Answer Key at the end of the Lesson Two Quiz.

Question 4

Some of the Medicaid quality measures address dental care and oral health. Specifically, there are two measures in the Child Core Set related to the Medicaid _____ Health Quality Improvement Initiative.

The answer to this question is found in Topic 2 and in the Lesson Two Quiz Answer Key at the end of the Lesson Two Quiz.

Question 5

Although many of the measures on the CAHPS Dental Plan Survey ask patients/customers about their experience with the dental insurance plan, some measures address the quality of dental care received. Which of the following is **not** one of those measures?

A. Overall Rating of Dental Care
B. Overall Rating of the Dentist
C. Overall Rating of the Dental Office Furnishings
D. Care from Dentists and Staff

The answer to this question is found in Topic 2 and in the Lesson Two Quiz Answer Key at the end of the Lesson Two Quiz.

Question 6

The American Dental Association (ADA) Dental Quality Alliance (DQA) is working on voluntary dental Practice Assessments quality measures to: "*assist practices in getting started with measuring towards quality improvement*".

A. True
B. False

The answer to this question is found in Topic 2 and in the Lesson Two Quiz Answer Key at the end of the Lesson Two Quiz.

Question 7

Some pharmacy-related accreditation programs such as the Community Pharmacy Practice Accreditation, Specialty Pharmacy Practice Accreditation Program, and Telehealth Pharmacy Practice Accreditation – include a requirement that the pharmacy operate a continuous quality improvement (CQI) program.

A. True
B. False

The answer to this question is found in Topic 3 and in the Lesson Two Quiz Answer Key at the end of the Lesson Two Quiz.

Question 8

Food and Drug Administration (FDA) approval is needed for drugs to legally enter the United States marketplace. Such approval constitutes the final steps of the Drug Development Process which has five steps. Which of the following is **not** one of the steps?

A. Discovery and Development
B. Packaging Focus Groups
C. Preclinical Research
D. Clinical Research

The answer to this question is found in Topic 3 and in the Lesson Two Quiz Answer Key at the end of the Lesson Two Quiz.

Question 9

Compounded drugs are not FDA approved: *"Quality requirements for compounded drugs differ depending on the setting where compounding occurs."*

A. True
B. False

The answer to this question is found in Topic 3 and in the Lesson Two Quiz Answer Key at the end of the Lesson Two Quiz.

Question 10

One of the best known quality ratings of medical/health plans is the National Committee for Quality Assurance (NCQA) Health Insurance Plan Ratings for commercial (private, Medicaid, and Medicare) insurance plans. Each rated plan is assigned an overall quality rating from 0 to 5 (five is highest) as well as a 0 to 5 quality rating in each of three categories. Which of the following is **not** one of the categories?

A. Treatment
B. Consumer Satisfaction
C. Profitability
D. Prevention

The answer to this question is found in Topic 4 and in the Lesson Two Quiz Answer Key at the end of the Lesson Two Quiz.

Question 11

Medicare provides Plan Quality and Performance Ratings. The Health Plan Quality Summary Rating gives information about the health plan's quality and performance. The ratings range from:

A. 1 to 10
B. 1 to 5
C. 5 to 10
D. 50 to 100

The answer to this question is found in Topic 4 and in the Lesson Two Quiz Answer Key at the end of the Lesson Two Quiz.

Question 12

The Pharmaceutical Care Management Association (PCMA) is the national association for PBMs who administer the prescription drug plans. PBM stands for:

A. Prescription Benefit Members
B. Pharmacy Buyer Majority
C. Prescription Buyer Membership
D. Pharmacy Benefit Managers

The answer to this question is found in Topic 4 and in the Lesson Two Quiz Answer Key at the end of the Lesson Two Quiz.

Question 13

In the United States, two major organizations have a national responsibility for public health quality (responsibility for health quality in the United States as a whole). Which of the following is **not** one of these organizations?

A. Surgeon General's Office in association with the Commissioned Corps of the United States Public Health Service (USPHS)
B. Centers for Disease Control and Prevention (CDC)
C. Department of Agriculture

The answer to this question is found in Topic 5 and in the Lesson Two Quiz Answer Key at the end of the Lesson Two Quiz.

Question 14

Which office has a focus *on "communicating "the best available scientific information to the public, using the position's platform to reach individuals where they live, work, and play and by issuing scientific documents on critical public health issues"*?

A. Office of the Press Secretary
B. Office of the Federal Aviation Association
C. Office of Environmental Investigation
D. Office of the Surgeon General

The answer to this question is found in Topic 5 and in the Lesson Two Quiz Answer Key at the end of the Lesson Two Quiz.

Question 15

The Healthy People initiative *"provides science-based, 10-year national objectives for improving the health of all Americans"*.

A. True
B. False

The answer to this question is found in Topic 5 and in the Lesson Two Quiz Answer Key at the end of the Lesson Two Quiz.

L2 Quiz Answer Key

Q1 = Healthcare; Q2 = B; Q3 = C; Q4 = Oral; Q5 = C; Q6 = A; Q7 = A; Q8 = B; Q9 = A; Q10 = C; Q11 = B; Q12 = D; Q13 = C; Q14 = D; Q15 = A

L2 "Create Your Own Healthcare Organization Quality Improvement Program"

In Lesson Four, you will *Design a Healthcare Organization Quality Improvement Program.* This competency development task requires that you synthesize content to create your own quality improvement program within a healthcare organization the way you would have things run in the best of all worlds. The type of healthcare organization is your choice (e.g., physical therapy office, dentist office, pharmacy, hospital, doctor's office).

Your synthesized information will be organized as an electronic spreadsheet. An example of a completed spreadsheet project is found in *Appendix B: Spreadsheet Example.* The spreadsheet is an artifact which you can circulate to colleagues or use for a talk or presentation event. Many people use Microsoft Excel for this purpose. However, there are many software options other than Excel. Some are available at no cost such as Calc [bib#198] which is part of LibreOffice [bib#199].

Eleven (11) content items and six (6) design items are suggested for the electronic spreadsheet task to develop competency. However, it is best not to wait until Lesson Four to begin to synthesize content to create your own quality improvement program within a healthcare organization. The earlier in your learning path that you begin this creation process, the better your own quality improvement program within a healthcare organization will be.

So in each lesson prior to Lesson Four, there will be an opportunity to begin to synthesize material – an opportunity to begin to create your own quality improvement program within a healthcare organization using material presented in that lesson. Of the eleven (11) suggested content items for the completed spreadsheet, one (1) is suggested for consideration in this lesson. It is posted below and includes an expanded description as well as an example. It is:

Suggested Spreadsheet Content Item 8
> A list of at least one measure that you use in your quality improvement program and a brief description as to why the measure was chosen.

There is no right or wrong answer to this question. It just has to be reasoned and make sense.

Example: The primary measure used by CHGH to measure patient/customer satisfaction to increase the quality of person-centeredness is the Adult Hospital Survey (HCAHPS [bib#223]) which "*asks people 18 and older about their experiences with medical, surgical, or obstetric care provided in an inpatient setting*".

This was chosen because it is used by more than 4000 hospitals in the United States which means it is reliable and valid and allows for benchmarking. Personnel from the Office of Quality Improvement also monitor reviews on such sites as Yelp and respond as necessary. Personnel also routinely visit patient/customer waiting areas and informally ask some patients/customers on a daily basis to provide informal feedback.

"The HCAHPS Survey contains 21 patient perspectives on care and patient rating items that encompass nine key topics: communication with doctors, communication with nurses, responsiveness of hospital staff, pain management, communication about medicines, discharge information, cleanliness of the hospital environment, quietness of the hospital environment, and transition of care.

The survey also includes four screener questions and seven demographic items, which are used for adjusting the mix of patients across hospitals and for analytical purposes. The survey is 32 questions in length.

There are four approved modes of administration for the CAHPS Hospital Survey: 1) Mail Only; 2) Telephone Only; 3) Mixed (mail followed by telephone); and 4) Active Interactive Voice Response (IVR). (Website Source of Quote [bib#392])

L2 Trivia Question and Virtual Field Trip

L2 Trivia Question

Almost everyone loves a trivia question – a question about a little known, but interesting, fun fact. Each lesson has one trivia question. The answer is in the Lesson Two Trivia Question Answer section.

Question:

Without question, the invention of the flush toilet increased the overall quality of population health through the reduction of disease – not to mention an increase in the overall quality of life. The invention of the flush toilet [bib#393] is credited to Sir John Harrington [bib#394] in 1592 when he installed a "*small downpipe through which water ran to flush the waste*".

However, since this was an open pipe, it did not keep out foul odors and sewer gases. This problem was solved in 1775. *Who solved the problem and what was the invention that solved the problem?*

L2 Trivia Question Answer

The answer to the Lesson Two trivia question is:

In 1775, Alexander Cummings received the first patent related to flush toilets for his invention of the S-shaped pipe/trap now commonly used with toilets to keep out odors and sewer gases

For more information, please see:

- The History of Sanitary Sewers [bib#395]
- Pondering the Privy: A History of Outhouses [bib#396]
- WPA Privy (1935-1943) [bib#397]

L2 Virtual Field Trip

Everyone loves a road trip/field trip so each lesson includes a "*virtual field trip*" to the often hidden places of interest on the web.

Lesson Two's virtual field trip is to the Corning Museum of Glass [bib#398] in Corning, New York. The Museum is "*dedicated to telling the story of a single material: glass ... the Museum's campus is home to the world's most comprehensive collection of glass, the world's foremost library on glass, and one of the top glassworking schools in the world ... The story of glass is a story about art, history, culture, technology, science, craft and design ... Nearly 50,000 objects representing more than 3,500 years of history [bib#399] are displayed in the galleries*".

Part of the Museum's collection contains jars used by druggists [bib#400] in past years to store ingredients for compounding. The Museum also has a collection of scientific glass [bib#401] – glass used by scientists such as chemists.

*****

> ***Video*** [bib#402]: *The video for the Lesson Two Virtual Field Trip – **The Corning Museum of Glass** – is a YouTube video produced by Smithsonian Magazine. It is a brief tour and overview of the Corning Museum of Glass.* The link for the video is: https://www.youtube.com/watch?v=JCMrSiXXEYQ

*****

Lesson Three (L3): Data Collection and Analysis Methodologies for Quality and Quality Improvement Measures in Healthcare Organizations

Note: The above picture is adapted from the one by Campaign Creators found on Unsplash
(https://unsplash.com/photos/pypeCEaJeZY)

L3 Competency Objective

This lesson provides an overview of data collection and analysis methodologies for quality and quality improvement measures in healthcare organizations. The competency objective is:

- Define the data collection and analysis methodologies for quality and quality improvement measures in healthcare organizations.

L3 Content and Discussion

This lesson provides an overview of data collection and analysis methodologies for quality and quality improvement measures in healthcare organizations. Upon successful completion of this lesson, you will be able to: define the data collection and analysis methodologies for quality and quality improvement measures in healthcare organizations. There are topic questions, a discussion question, a quiz, a trivia question, and a field trip. The lesson should take 4 - 6 hours of work to successfully complete. There are also videos which provide supplemental content which can help you better define your personal learning path. There are many wonderful videos in the public domain which are relevant to the topics in this book.

This lesson addresses five (5) topics organized as questions. An answer for the health care delivery system you are proposing is provided for each question to help you organize your thinking and come to your own conclusions and answer consistent with your personal learning goal. The questions/topics for Lesson Three are:

1. What are the types of data from quality measures used in healthcare organizations?

2. What are the methodologies used to collect and analyze data for quality measures in healthcare organizations?

3. What are the Cause-and-Effect Diagram and Check Sheet tools for quality in healthcare organizations?

4. What are Control Charts and the Histogram tools for quality in healthcare organizations?

5. What are the Pareto Chart, Scatter Diagram, and Stratification tools for quality in healthcare organizations?

L3 Topic 1 (T1). What are the types of data from quality measures used in healthcare organizations?

One of the first steps in healthcare organization quality improvement is deciding what measures and data will be part of that quality improvement program. Clearly, any healthcare organization in any quality improvement effort can choose any quality measure it wishes, collect the data for that measure in any way it chooses, and analyze that data in any manner it wishes. However, it is more productive if the healthcare organization implements that quality improvement effort consistent with and using known standards for measures, data collection, and data analysis.

Lesson One, Topic 5 discussed the characteristics (criteria) for a good, accepted quality measure. For example, National Quality Forum (NQF [bib#183]), Measure Evaluation Criteria [bib#184] states that such a quality measure should have the following characteristics:

1. Importance to Measure and Report
2. Scientific Acceptability of Measure Properties
3. Feasibility
4. Usability and Use
5. Comparison to Related or Competing Measures

Once a healthcare organization chooses the specific quality measures to be used, that organization has to determine, collect, and analyze the data associated with that measure.

This section addresses:

- Types of Quality Data
- Quality Data Documentation

L3-T1. Types of Quality Data

The data for healthcare organization quality measures are of two general types: qualitative and quantitative. These are the same types which exist for all data. It is important to understand and choose the type of data to be collected carefully since the type of analyses which can be done is related to the type of data.

Qualitative data include descriptions, stories, images, and opinions in their entirety – exactly as they were created (e.g., exactly as written, exactly as spoken). Examples include the transcripts or recordings of individual interviews with patients/customers as well as those of participants in a patient satisfaction focus group discussion. Qualitative data are not "*analyzed*" in the statistical sense, although they can be analyzed using qualitative analysis methods. Qualitative data can be analyzed, for example, in the sense of determining whether there are common themes across the material from different people. There is software which helps a researcher accomplish this task (e.g., text analysis). Examples of free software which do this are:

- QDA MINER LITE [bib#403]
- Coding Analysis Toolkit (CAT) [bib#404]

More information about qualitative research can be found in journals such as Qualitative Research (QRJ) [bib#405] which "*publishes original research and review articles on the methodological diversity and multi-disciplinary focus of qualitative research*".

Another journal is Qualitative Health Research (QHR) [bib#406] which is a "*peer-reviewed monthly journal that provides an international, interdisciplinary forum to enhance health care and further the development and understanding of qualitative research in health-care settings*".

Quantitative data are numerical data. Such data are able to be modeled and analyzed statistically. Most data used to measure quality and quality improvement are quantitative. Generally, quantitative data are considered to have four levels [bib#407]: nominal, ordinal, interval, or ratio. The definition of these levels is credited to Stanley Smith Stevens [bib#408] in his 1946 publication entitled *On the Theory and Scales of Measurement* [bib#409].

1. Nominal Data represent categories (discrete, categorical data) of a measure which can be assigned a number, but the number (usually an integer like 1,

2, ...) is "*meaningless*". The number itself has no numerical measurement value. It is a category.

1.1. One example is the data for the Measure: Healthcare Organization Department. Each department in the healthcare organization can be assigned a number (e.g., Emergency Department = 1, Surgical Department = 2), but the number is meaningless (e.g., Emergency Department is not less than the Surgical Department and the numbers could have been reversed).

2. Ordinal Data represent categories (discrete, categorical data) of a measure which can be assigned a number (usually an integer like 1, 2, ...) which has meaning in terms of the order. A higher number is, for example, "*more*" of the measure than is a lower number, but it is not clear how much more. The number itself has no numerical measurement value. It is a category.

2.1. One example is the data for the Measure: Patient Satisfaction. If three possible patient response categories are allowed (e.g., Dissatisfied, Neutral, Satisfied) then each can be assigned a number which reflects the general order of patient satisfaction (Dissatisfied = 1, Neutral = 2, Satisfied= 3). However, the number 3 does not indicate how satisfied the patient is with the healthcare organization or how it differs in amount from either Neutral or Dissatisfied.

3. Interval Data represent a measurement (continuous data) of a measure. It can have other than integer values and the "*distance between*" – the "*amount between*" each measurement is equal. For example, the distance/amount between 1 and 2 is the same as between 15 and 16. However, interval data has no true zero; there is no true absence of the measure.

3.1. The common example for this level is the Fahrenheit temperature scale. It is applicable to the Measure: Patient Temperature. The difference in patient temperature between 95 degrees and 96 degrees is the same as the difference between 100 degrees and 101 degrees. A temperature of 0 degrees, however, does not mean that there is no

Patient Temperature Measure; it means the temperature of the patient is 0 degrees.

3.2. And 0 degrees on the Fahrenheit temperature scale is different from that [bib#410] on the Celsius temperature scale (no true 0 for the measure). Zero degrees on the Fahrenheit scale is equal to -17.8 degrees on the Celsius scale; 0 degrees on the Celsius scale is equal to 32 degrees on the Fahrenheit scale.

4. Ratio Data represent a measurement (continuous data) of a measure. It can have other than integer values and the "*distance between*" – the "*amount between*" each measurement is equal. In this sense, Ratio Data are similar to Interval Data. However, Ratio Data has a true zero; there is a true absence of the measure. Because a true zero exists, a ratio of the data has meaning. It is appropriate to say, for example, that 5 is half of 10 and that 10 is twice 5.

4.1. Classic examples of Ratio Data measures are height and weight. For healthcare organization quality measures, one example is the number of patients seen during a specific time period. If the measure data value is 0, then, in fact, there were no patients seen. If one healthcare organization sees 10 patients and other sees 5, then the 10-patient organization sees twice as many patients as the 5-patient organization.

There are many software tools (discussed more later in the lesson) which can be used to model and statistically analyze quantitative data. Examples include:

- Excel [bib#411]
- LibreOffice Calc [bib#412]
- SAS [bib#413]
- The R Project for Statistical Computing [bib#414]
- ArcGIS [bib#415]

L3-T1. Quality Data Documentation

It is important for any healthcare organization to document in detail the quality measures and data used for quality improvement. If the organization is using measures developed and data collected by others (for the organization's quality improvement or benchmarking), it is important to understand the details of those measures and collected data.

Many consider a data document and data to be the foundation [bib#416] on which quality and quality improvement are built. The details of quality improvement lie in an understanding of the data used for quality improvement. Such details for a dataset of measures (variables) and data are usually contained in a document called data documentation (or data dictionary or codebook).

Such a document [bib#417] "*describes the contents, structure, and layout of a data collection ... information intended to be complete and self-explanatory for each variable in a data file*". Specifically, such data documentation often contains (at a minimum):

- Measure/Variable Name
- Data Type/Level (e.g., quantitative, ratio)
- Valid Data for the Measure (e.g., range of 0 to 100; 1, 2, 3)
- Any Value Associated with the Valid Data (e.g., 1= Fair, 2=Good, 3=Excellent)

A healthcare organization must ensure that all quality measures and associated data are documented and that the documentation is updated as needed so that everyone involved in the quality improvement program can easily understand the measures and data underlying the quality improvement (QI) program. If existing data collected elsewhere are used in the QI program, then the data documentation for that dataset should be obtained and made available to all so that the external data can be properly understood in relationship to the internal QI measures and data.

Examples of the data documentation for datasets (measures and data) which might be used by a healthcare organization in its QI program (e.g., for benchmarking) can be found at:

- Medicare Current Beneficiary Survey (MCBS) Data Documentation and Codebooks [bib#418]

- National Hospital Discharge Survey (NHDS), NHDS - Downloadable documentation via ftp [bib#419]

- National Hospital Ambulatory Medical Care Survey (NHAMCS) Downloadable Documentation, NHAMCS, 1992-2016 [bib#420]

- Improving the Measurement of Surgical Site Infection Risk Stratification/Outcome Detection: Appendix C. Data Dictionary [bib#421]

Other data documentation examples can be found in the rules and guidelines for depositing data in a data repository. A list of data repositories can be found at re3data.org [bib#422] as well as Open Access Directory [bib#423]. One data repository example is the Health and Medical Care Archive (HMCA [bib#424]). Data submitted to this repository must comply with the Inter-University Consortium for Political and Social Research (ICPSR [bib#425]), Guide to Social Science Data Preparation and Archiving [bib#426] and complete the ICPSR Electronic Data Deposit Form [bib#427].

*****

Video [bib#428]*: The video for Topic 1 – **ICPSR 101: Why Should I Cite Data?** – is a YouTube video produced by the Inter-University Consortium for Political and Social Research (ICPSR). This video discusses why data used for any research or project should be cited in presentations about that research/project. The link for the video is:*
https://www.youtube.com/watch?v=jiCZKV-alC0

*****

Additional examples of data documentation are available in journals whose published articles focus on data and datasets such as:

- Data - Open Access Journal [bib#429] whose intent is "*enhancing data transparency and reusability. The journal publishes in two sections: a section on the collection, treatment and analysis methods of data in science; a section publishing descriptions of scientific and scholarly datasets (one dataset per paper)*".

- Data-In-Brief Journal [bib#430] which "*provides a way for researchers to easily share and reuse each other's datasets by publishing data articles that: Thoroughly describe your data, facilitating reproducibility ...*"

- Scientific Data Journal [bib#431] which is for "*descriptions of scientifically valuable datasets, and research that advances the sharing and reuse of scientific data*".

Additional resources relevant to this topic are:

- Create a Codebook [bib#432]
- Codebook Cookbook [bib#433]
- How to Make a Data Dictionary [bib#434]
- Documenting Data [bib#435]
- Data Documentation and Metadata [bib#436]

L3 Topic 2 (T2). What are the methodologies used to collect and analyze data for quality measures in healthcare organizations?

Once a healthcare organization has decided which measures and data to include in the quality improvement (QI) program, the healthcare organization must decide on the methodologies to be used collecting that data and analyzing that data.

This section addresses:

- Quality Data Collection Methodologies
- Quality Data Analysis Methodologies

L 3-T2. Quality Data Collection Methodologies

Healthcare organizations usually collect data for quality improvement (QI) programs using three basic methodologies: surveys (e.g., survey of patients/customers), internal healthcare organization records (e.g., Electronic Medical Records), and external relevant databases (e.g., national data on a topic for benchmarking purposes). Sometimes individual interviews or focus groups (e.g., interview or focus group with patients/customers to discuss patient/customer satisfaction).

In the best of all possible worlds, the data for a QI program would be collected in a manner consistent with accepted data collection standards; accepted data collection methodologies (e.g., accepted experimental design standards). Using such standards ensures that the results of the analyses of that data – the conclusions drawn from the data – are ones which can be trusted for the purposes of making decisions about QI. Making and implementing QI decisions can be resource intensive. Any healthcare organization wants to ensure that those resource expenditures are focused on an accurate (trusted) description of the quality in the focus area.

Unfortunately, for many reasons, the use of accepted data collection standards/methodologies is not always possible in real-time quality improvement in a healthcare organization. This situation is discussed later in the lesson. For the moment, it worthwhile to review what the "*gold standard*" of data collection standards/methodologies is.

For qualitative data (e.g. descriptions, images), there are three basic qualitative data collection forms/methodologies: 1) interview (individual, focus group), 2) observation (individual, group, location), and 3) document analysis (content analysis). Which data are collected depends on the overall purpose of the qualitative study. That is, which data are collected is guided by the qualitative research design to be used. A good summary of qualitative research designs can be found at Research Rundowns: Qualitative Research Design [bib#437]. Examples include:

- Phenomenology – the researcher analyzes an event (phenomenon) and its impact from the perspective of those who experienced it (collected data must relate to the event)

- Grounded Theory – the researcher analyzes data on a specific topic to identify any common themes which can lead to research questions for further study analysis (collected data must relate to the topic)

- Case Study – the researcher analyzes an entity (e.g., concept, organization, person) from multiple perspectives (collected data must relate to the entity)

Qualitative research is not commonly used in quality improvement although some argue that it should be used more in healthcare organizations. One example is the discussion in the article entitled *Qualitative methods in research on healthcare quality* [bib#438].

For quantitative data, the usual data collection forms/methodologies are surveys/questionnaires, direct observations/measurements, and use of existing records/data. Which data are collected is guided by quantitative research designs.

One aspect of these designs is whether the chosen measures and method of determining the data for that measure are reliable and valid. The National Quality Forum (NQF), for example, only approves quality measures for use which meet the Measure Evaluation Criteria [bib#184]. One NQF approval evaluation criterion is *Reliability and Validity – Scientific Acceptability of Measure Properties* which is the: "*Extent to which the measure, as specified, produces consistent (reliable) and credible (valid) results about the quality of care when implemented*".

This topic is discussed in the NQF document entitled *Guidance for Measure Testing and Evaluating Scientific Acceptability of Measure Properties* [bib#439]. Special care must be taken with surveys used for quality [bib#440] improvement to ensure that the questions produce measures and data which are reliable and valid.

Another aspect of these designs is choosing the specific people, records, etc. from which to collect data. This is usually called constructing the sample or sampling strategy. Rarely are there enough resources to obtain data from every single person, record, etc. who has data for that measure. For example, in testing a new drug to treat a specific disease, only a sample of those people with that disease is included in the test. Everyone (every single known person with the disease) with the disease (the population of those with the disease) is not included.

The sample must be chosen in a way that maximizes the probability that the results determined by the data of those in the sample are the same as if the results were based on data from everyone with that disease (data from the entire population). Examples of sampling strategies used for quality [bib#441] improvement include:

- Random sampling [bib#442] – sample is chosen randomly with each unit in the population having an equal chance of being selected for the sample; sometimes this is implemented by assigning each unit in the population a number and then using a Random Number Generator (RNG) [bib#443] to choose the sample

- Stratified random sampling [bib#444] – the population is separated/organized into groups (stratified) and then a sample chosen randomly within each group/strata

- Systematic sampling [bib#445] – the sample is chosen from the population according to a system – a systematized rule (e.g., data obtained from every fourth unit)

Another aspect – once the measures and sampling strategy have been decided – is deciding from how many people, records, etc. data are to be collected (e.g., 10 patients/customers, 100 patients/customers). This aspect is called the sample size. The sample size must be large enough for the researcher to be confident that the collected data are representative of the whole population. How much data are needed depends in large measure how much "*confidence*" the researcher needs. That "*confidence*" is defined by confidence level [bib#446], confidence interval [bib#447], and margin of error [bib#448]. The sample size is often calculated using on online sample size generator [bib#449].

Another aspect is the experimental design. The classic, true experimental design [bib#450] includes a randomized sample, randomized assignment to experimental and control groups, as well as researcher control over the independent and dependent variables (a.k.a., randomized control trial). In this design, it is possible for the researcher to determine which independent variables affect the dependent variable and to what extent. One example of a true experimental design contains a pre-test, post-test, a randomly selected and assigned experimental group, a randomly selected and assigned control group, and an intervention/treatment with the experimental group.

Experimental designs which are not "*true*" – which contain some, but not all of the characteristics of a classic, true experimental design – are often called quasi-experimental designs [bib#451]. One example of a quasi-experimental design is a pre-test, post-test, experimental group (not randomly chosen, not randomly assigned), a control group (not randomly chosen, not randomly assigned), and an intervention/treatment with the experimental group.

Although quality improvement programs can and must use valid and reliable measures, it is often difficult in a real-time, ongoing program to use "*gold standard*" sampling and experimental design data collection strategies. The "*gold standard*" examines one factor (one intervention, one change) at a time and draws conclusions about that factor before examining another factor. This "*gold standard*" is called, in quality improvement, the One–Factor–at–a–Time (OFAT) strategy.

Although OFAT is sometimes used in quality improvement, a data collection strategy called Design of Experiments (DOE) [bib#452] is often used. The difference between OFAT and DOE is that DOE can collect data and draw conclusions on more than one factor at a time. The basic strategy of DOE is to:

1. Identify the factors to be examined.

2. Determine the reasonable high and reasonable low value for each factor.

3. Run an experiment/test which examines the effect of each factor at its low and at its high value.

4. Analyze the results of all of the experiments/tests to determine the effect of each factor and their interaction.

For example, assume two factors are considered important in the quality of a cake: sugar and vanilla. A reasonable low level of sugar for the cake is 0.5 cups; a reasonable high level for the cake is 2 cups. A reasonable low level of vanilla for the cake is 0.5 teaspoons and a reasonable high level for the cake is 1.5 teaspoons.

In the OFAT strategy, four experiments/tests would be done with an analysis of the results done after each individual experiment and conclusions drawn about the factor and the factor level:

1. **Experiment 1:** 0.5 cups of sugar (low) while the rest of the recipe remains the same; results obtained, analysis done, and conclusions drawn

2. **Experiment 2:** 2.0 cups of sugar (high) while the rest of the recipe remains the same; results obtained, analysis done and conclusions drawn

3. **Experiment 3:** 0.5 teaspoons of vanilla (low) while the rest of the recipe remains the same; results obtained, analysis done and conclusions drawn

4. **Experiment 4:** 1.5 teaspoons of vanilla (high) while the rest of the recipe remains the same; results obtained, analysis done and conclusions drawn

In the DOE strategy, four experiments would be done with an analysis of the results done only after all four experiments have been completed; the results of all four experiments are in the same analysis and conclusions are drawn about the effect of each factor, factor level, and their interaction.

1. **Experiment 1:** 0.5 cups of sugar (low), 0.5 teaspoons of vanilla (low) while the rest of the recipe remains the same; results obtained

2. **Experiment 2:** 0.5 cups of sugar (low), 1.5 teaspoons of vanilla (high) while the rest of the recipe remains the same; results obtained

3. **Experiment 3:** 2.0 cups of sugar (high), 0.5 teaspoons of vanilla (low) while the rest of the recipe remains the same; results obtained

4. **Experiment 4:** 2.0 cups of sugar (high), 1.5 teaspoons of vanilla (high) while the rest of the recipe remains the same; results obtained

5. **Analysis** done using the results of all four experiments and conclusions drawn

In the OFAT strategy, the analysis and conclusions are only about the effect of one factor at a time (either sugar or vanilla). In the DOE strategy, the analysis and conclusions are about both factors and their interaction. Not only does the DOE strategy provide more quality information, it is a faster process than the OFAT strategy for the purpose of quality improvement.

The origin of the DOE strategy is credited to Ronald Fisher [bib#453], a statistician, and his work on ways to improve agricultural crop quality. He published a book entitled *Design of Experiments* [bib#454] in 1935. He developed the Analysis of Variance (ANOVA) which he first used in his 1921 publication entitled *On the "Probable Error" of a Coefficient of Correlation Deduced from a Small Sample* [bib#455]. He also developed the Fisher's z-distribution [bib#456] now used as the F-distribution [bib#457]. Fisher's 1925 publication entitled *Statistical Methods for Research Workers* [bib#458] is considered by many to be a classic work on statistics.

Additional information can be found in the following resources:

- Understanding Design of Experiments [bib#459]
- What Is Design of Experiments (DOE)? [bib#460]
- Introduction to Design of Experiments (DOE) [bib#461]
- Design of Experiments – A Primer [bib#462]
- Experimental and Quasi-Experimental Designs for Research [bib#463] by Donald T. Campbell and Julian C. Stanley (an old book, but a timeless classic)
- A First Course in Probability [bib#464] by Sheldon Ross (a book on probability with clear explanations)

- History of Probability [bib#465]
- SAGE Research Methods [bib#466]

OFAT for quality can be found in healthcare organizations especially in the areas of drug discovery/development and clinical trials [bib#315]. DOE is also used. However, it is difficult to conduct real-time, "*gold standard*" experiments related to quality in a healthcare organization. A healthcare organization may not be able to realistically regulate those factors considered important to quality in a day-to-day, real-time situation. It is difficult to meet any "*gold standard*" for data collection.

For example, a hospital may send a survey to discharged patients, but there is no realistic way to make a patient return a completed survey. Therefore, any conclusions based on the returned surveys may not reflect the reality of overall patient satisfaction with the quality of the hospital. Another example is that a hospital may believe that the number of patients in an emergency room affect the quality of health care delivered in the emergency room. However, there is no realistic way for the hospital to regulate the number of patients arriving at and being treated in the emergency room.

For this reason, quality improvement in healthcare organizations often relies on models (simulations) for "*running*" DOE experiments. Such models are only effective if they accurately reflect the business processes of the healthcare organization. A model which can manipulate the number of patients in an emergency room and their relationship to quality must be built to reflect the real-time processes at work in the emergency room. Quality improvement, therefore, begins with a thorough understanding of current healthcare organization processes.

Additional information can be found in the following resources:

- Tests of Change: Simulated Design of Experiments in Healthcare Delivery [bib#467]

- DOE Use in the Health Care Industry [bib#468]

- National Institutes of Health (NIH), Rigor and Responsibility [bib#469]

- Food and Drug Administration (FDA) Drug Study Designs, Information Sheet [bib#470]

L 3-T2. Quality Data Analysis Methodologies

Once the data have been collected, they need to be analyzed and conclusions drawn. At some level, any healthcare organization can use any analysis method it chooses. It can construct a new method. At another level, it is productive to use analyses which are well recognized for producing results on which healthcare organizations can rely for making quality and quality improvement decisions.

One example of quality method constructed by an organization is the method associated with rankings. For example, the methods used to compute the U.S. News healthcare organization quality rankings can be found at its FAQ: How and Why We Rank and Rate Hospitals [bib#471] website, specifically Methodology: US News & World Report 2018-2019 Best Hospitals Specialty Rankings [bib#472].

Another example is the method used to generate the Centers for Medicare and Medicaid Services (CMS) Hospital Compare overall hospital star [bib#473] ratings. The comprehensive methodology report for the calculation of the star ratings is found at the QualityNet, Overall Hospital Ratings, Methodology [bib#474] website. It is important to note that there are many hospitals which disagree with the methodology.

The criticisms center on the fact that the ratings methodology does not use the same number of measures in the rating of every hospital and that some important measures (e.g., socioeconomic situation of the local area) are not included. Critics argue that such methodology puts teaching hospitals as a whole at a quality disadvantage and is not an accurate reflection of the quality of individual hospitals.

Additional information can be found in the following resources:

- CMS star ratings disproportionately benefit specialty hospitals, data show [bib#475]

- 3 Reasons CMS Star Ratings Are Misleading [bib#476]

- CMS Star Ratings Met with Criticism in Academic Medicine Community [bib#477]

- Three top criticisms against CMS' overall hospital star ratings [bib#478]

- Patient Characteristics and Differences in Hospital Readmission Rates [bib#479]

- CMS star ratings criticized for ignoring socioeconomic factors [bib#480]

- My Favorite Slide: Why Five-Star Hospitals May Be More Closely Related to Five-Star Restaurants than Innate Quality [bib#481]

So clearly any organization can construct any quality measure and methodology it wishes, but others may not agree with it. For this reason many organizations use well known and accepted analysis methods for quality measures and data. Such methods include analytics, descriptive statistics, inferential statistics and sometimes spatial statistics. There are many fine resources on each of these statistics types – which are used for a wide variety of purposes not just quality – so they will not be further discussed in this course. Some of the resources are:

- The R Project for Statistical Computing [bib#414]
- SAS – Industries – Health Care Analytics [bib#482]
- IBM SPSS Software [bib#483]
- History of Statistics [bib#484]
- ESRI – Industries – Health and Human Services [bib#485]
- National Center for Health Statistics (NCHS) Data Visualization Gallery [bib#486]
- GIS and Public Health at CDC [bib#487]
- Principles of Epidemiology in Public Health Practice [bib#488]
- Discovering Statistics Using R [bib#489] – a book by Andy Field, Jeremy Miles, and Zoe Field
- Computational Handbook of Statistics [bib#490] – a book by James L. Bruning and B.L. Kintz (an old book, but a timeless classic)
- Spatial Statistics Journal [bib#491]
- American Statistical Association (ASA) [bib#492]

*****

Video [bib#493]*: The video for Topic 2 – **The beauty of data visualization** – is a YouTube video produced by TED. This video discusses ways to turn complex data and datasets into an easier-to-understand visual presentation. The link for the video is:* https://www.youtube.com/watch?v=pLqjQ55tz-U

*****

Although any of the data collection and analysis methodologies discussed above can be used by any healthcare organization for a quality improvement (QI) program, there are some which are considered an essential part of any part of any QI program – methodologies with which every QI professional should be aware. These are worthy of further discussion in a course on quality improvement in healthcare organizations. They are discussed in the next sections of the lesson.

L3 Topic 3 (T3). What are the Cause-and-Effect Diagram and Check Sheet tools for quality in healthcare organizations?

There are tools and methods commonly found in quality improvement (QI) work with which any QI professional should be familiar. Some of these are referred to as The Seven Basic Tools of Quality (or The Basic Seven or The First Seven). Kaoru Ishikawa [bib#494] is credited with development of this list of seven quality tools. The tools are:

1. Cause-and-Effect Diagram
2. Check Sheet
3. Control Charts
4. Histogram
5. Pareto Chart
6. Scatter Diagram
7. Stratification.

A comprehensive discussion of these tools and many other tools, methods, and issues in quality improvement can be found in The Quality Toolbox [bib#495] – a book by Nancy Tague.

This section addresses:

- Cause-and-Effect Diagram
- Check Sheet

L 3-T3. Cause-and-Effect Diagram

The development of the cause-and-effect diagram is credited to Kaoru Ishikawa [bib#494]. The diagram is also known as the Ishikawa chart or fishbone chart. The purpose of the diagram is to visually represent the possible causes for a quality problem situation (effect) which is the focus of quality improvement (QI).

The process of developing the diagram helps those involved in the QI program organize their thinking and understand the processes affecting the quality problem situation of focus. The diagram itself adds visual clarity to the discussion and QI efforts. The diagram visualizes a quality problem situation (the effect) and the factors which impact it (the causes of the effect). Building a cause-and-effect diagram usually involves four (4) steps:

Step 1. Briefly define the effect (quality problem situation) which is the focus of the QI effort (e.g., low level of patient/customer satisfaction); this definition takes the form of a brief quality problem statement.

Step 2. Briefly define the major causes/factors affecting the quality problem situation (effect). It is suggested, although not required, that as an initial definition the causes be organized [bib#496] into four categories for service industries (The 4 Ps) and six categories for manufacturing industries (The 6 Ms).

The suggested categories for service industries (The 4 Ps) are:

- Policies
- Procedures
- People
- Plant/Technology (Facilities, Equipment)

The suggested categories for manufacturing industries (The 6 Ms) are:

- Machines
- Methods
- Materials
- Measurements
- Mother Nature (Environment)
- Manpower (People)

Step 3. Briefly define each major cause in more detail in order to find root causes of the effect. This process is sometimes accomplished through use of a process called the Five Whys Analysis [bib#497]. The process asks "Why" repeatedly to get to the root cause of the major cause of the problem, and thus, the root cause of the problem. Usually identifying the root cause takes five or fewer "whys". The Centers for Medicare and Medicaid (CMS) provides the following example [bib#498] of a set of "whys":

"*Here is an everyday example of using the Five Whys to determine a root cause:*

Problem statement – your car gets a flat tire on your way to work.

1. *Why did you get a flat tire?*
   - *You ran over nails in your garage.*

2. *Why were there nails on the garage floor?*
   - *The box of nails on the shelf was wet; the box fell apart and nails fell from the box onto the floor. **

3. *Why was the box of nails wet?*
   - *There was a leak in the roof and it rained hard last night. (Root cause=leak in the roof)*

* *IF YOU STOPPED HERE AND "SOLVED" THE PROBLEM BY SWEEPING UP THE NAILS, YOU WOULD HAVE MISSED THE ROOT CAUSE OF THE PROBLEM."*

Step 4. Iterate on Steps 1 - 3 gathering more information from all those who might have information on the effect, major causes, and detailed (root) causes, until the QI team is relatively confident of the information.

Once Step 4 is complete, visualize the information from Step 1, Step 2, and Step 3 by placing the information on a cause-and-effect (fishbone, Ishikawa) diagram/chart. This diagram looks like a fish with the effect problem statement at the "*head*" of the fish and the causes forming the "*skeleton*" – the bones – of the fish. Templates for the cause-and-effect diagram can be found in both Word and Excel at the links below:

- Fishbone Template, Word [bib#499]
- How to Create a Fishbone Diagram in Word [bib#500]
- Fishbone Template, Excel [bib#501]
- Fishbone (Cause & Effect Diagram) Excel Template [bib#502]
- Fishbone Diagram Template in Excel [bib#503]

The QI team should iterate on the diagram as many times as is necessary and, if need be, go back to Step 1 through Step 4.

The application of the cause-and-effect diagram to healthcare organization quality improvement is illustrated in the Centers for Medicare and Medicaid Services (CMS) resource entitled *How to Use the Fishbone Tool for Root Cause Analysis* [bib#504] (RCA) which is provided as part of the CMS Process Tool Framework [bib#505] to implement the basic principles of Quality Assurance and Performance Improvement (QAPI [bib#506]).

Other examples of healthcare organization application of the cause-and-effect diagram can be found at:

- Minnesota Department of Health, Fishbone Diagram [bib#507]

- Improhealth Collaborative, Fishbone Diagram [bib#508]

- West Central Public Health Initiative, Immunization Quality Improvement Project [bib#509]

- Using a Fishbone Diagram to Assess and Remedy Barriers to Cervical Cancer Screening in Your Healthcare Setting [bib#510]

*****

Video [bib#511]*: The video for Topic 3 – **Fishbone Diagram** – is a YouTube video produced by the Western Region Public Health Training Center. This video discusses the use of Fishbone Diagrams to improve the quality of public health. The link for the video is:*
https://www.youtube.com/watch?v=2rLB-1z9cPY

*****

Additional information can be found in the following resources:

- Fishbone (Ishikawa) Diagram [bib#512]
- Fishbone Diagram Tutorial [bib#513]
- The Cause and Effect (a.k.a. Fishbone) Diagram [bib#514]

L3-T3.   Check Sheet

The check sheet is a data collection tool to track "*effects*" – to track when, where, etc a specific quality problem occurs. The check sheet is a spreadsheet with the effects to be tracked listed vertically in the first column. The when, where, etc. of interest are listed horizontally in the first row. A check mark is placed in the intersection of the effect and the relevant when, where, etc. at the time the effect occurs.

An effective check sheet requires that the Quality Improvement (QI) team generate a complete list of all of the effects of interest as well as a complete list of all of the conditions under which that effect occurs. One or more individuals then observes (watches for) the occurrence of the listed effects and the conditions under which they occur and marks the check sheet accordingly.

For example, suppose the effect of interest is *"Electronic Medical Record (EMR) system too slow"* where the QI team defines *"too slow"* (e.g., end user perceives it as slow, takes more than 5 seconds for a page to load). And the effect occurrence of interest is the general time of day (e.g., morning, afternoon). The QI team could then ask each person using the EMR to mark a check sheet for one week whenever the EMR is too slow. The resulting check for one person might look like:

Effect	Morning	Afternoon	Total
EMR Too Slow	xxxxxxxx = 8	xxx = 3	11

In the above example, over the course of the data collection period, the person responsible for this check sheet noticed and recorded eight (8) times the EMR was too slow in the morning (each check mark represents one occurrence) and three (3) times it was too slow in the afternoon for a total of 11 times/occurrences during the data collection period. Each check sheet should also contain identifying information [bib#515] such as:

- Who filled out the check sheet
- What was collected (e.g., the definition of the EMR being too slow)
- Where the collection took place (e.g., which computer was being used at the time)
- When the collection took place (e.g., specific week data were collected, definition of morning)
- Why the data were collected

The Minnesota Department of Health provides an example of a check sheet at its Check Sheet [bib#516] website.

Additional information can be found in the following resources:

- ASQ Check Sheet [bib#517]
- Using Check Sheets to Improve Data Analysis [bib#518]

L3 Topic 4 (T4). What are Control Charts and the Histogram tools for quality in healthcare organizations?

As mentioned in Topic 3, there are tools and methods commonly found in quality improvement (QI) work with which any QI professional should be familiar. They are: 1) cause-and-effect diagram, 2) check sheet, 3) control charts, 4) histogram, 5) pareto chart, 6) scatter diagram, and 7) stratification. The first two (cause-and-effect diagram, check sheet) were discussed in Topic 3. This section addresses:

- Control Charts
- Histogram

L 3-T4. Control Charts

A control chart can be considered a monitoring system which indicates when action needs to be taken. As long as no action needs to be taken the situation is considered under control. The basic purpose of the control chart is to determine when events are under control and when they are not; when organizational processes can continue as is and when changes (interventions) need to be made.

For example, you may set your home thermostat to 70 degrees. The temperature sensor in your thermostat monitors the temperature. As long as the temperature is 70 degrees, the thermostat *"sees"* the situation as under control. If the temperature rises to 71 degrees, the situation is out of control and action must be taken – the air conditioner turns on. If the temperature falls to 69 degrees, the situation is out of control and action must be taken – the heat turns on. In control chart language, simplistically speaking, 70 degrees is called the Center Line (CL) while 71 degrees is called Upper Control Limit (UCL) and 69 degrees is called the Lower Control Limit (LCL).

A healthcare example might involve the number of patients/customers arriving in the Emergency Room. If, over time, the number of people arriving averages 15 people per day (Center Line, CL), then the situation may be considered under control and no change to existing Emergency Room processes is needed. If more than 20 people arrive (Upper Control Limit, UCL), then the situation is out of control and action must be taken (e.g., call in more Emergency

Room staff). If less than 10 people arrive (Lower Control Limit, LCL), then the situation is out of control and action must be taken (e.g., reassigns Emergency Room staff to other locations or send them home).

The visual display of the two scenarios just discussed is a control chart. The American Society for Quality (ASQ) defines a control chart [bib#519] as:

"*a graph used to study how a process changes over time. Data are plotted in time order. A control chart always has a central line for the average, an upper line for the upper control limit and a lower line for the lower control limit. These lines are determined from historical data. By comparing current data to these lines, you can draw conclusions about whether the process variation is consistent (in control) or is unpredictable (out of control, affected by special causes of variation)*".

In the above examples, 70 degrees and 15 people per day equal the control chart Central Line (CL) for the average. The upper line for the Upper Control Limit (UCL) is 71 degrees and 20 people. The lower line for the Lower Control Limit (LCL) is 69 degrees and 10 people. Once an accurate control chart is generated for a situation, problems (out of control situations) can be corrected immediately (in real-time) as they occur. A real-time correction (action) occurs immediately at 71 degrees, 20 people, 69 degrees, and 10 people.

The placement of the average (Center Line, CL), Upper Control Limit (UCL) and Lower Control Limit (LCL) in the above examples is over-simplified. In reality, both the UCL and LCL are calculated [bib#520] values which are usually three standard deviations [bib#521] from the average.

The development of the control chart [bib#522] is credited to Walter Andrew Shewhart [bib#523] and his 1924 memo addressing the manufacturing of telephone equipment. The memo addressed ways to ensure that the telephone equipment did not have a high probability of failure once installed by defining statistically normal/acceptable variations in the manufactured product (in-control) and unacceptable ones (out-of-control variations) which would likely result in failure of the equipment after installation). Shewhart's work is also considered the foundation of Statistical Process Control (SPC [bib#524]) .

Many people use the terms Statistical Quality Control (SQC) and Statistical Process Control (SPC) interchangeably. Some QI professionals, however, make a distinction between Statistical Quality Control (SQC) and Statistical Process Control (SPC). ASQ, for example, states that:

"Statistical quality control (SQC) is the application of ... statistical and analytical tools ... to monitor process outputs (dependent variables). Statistical process control (SPC) is the application of the same ... tools to control process inputs (independent variables)".

ISIXSIGMA [bib#525] states that:

"Some prefer SQC because the idea of "quality" is larger and more encompassing than that of "process." Others counter this by pointing out that the term "process" is problematic by nature, whereas a focus on "quality" is symptomatic in character. Still others looked at SQC as the management version of SPC. The bottom line s simple – both approaches get the job done".

*****

Video [bib#526]: *The video for Topic 4 –* **Honda Statistical Process Control** *– is a YouTube video produced by Operations Management. This video discusses how Honda Motor Corporation uses Statistical Process Control to monitor Quality. The link for the video is:*
https://www.youtube.com/watch?v=Sdj-8ZBYYmo

*****

There are many different types of control charts. Each has the same purpose; they each have the same basic elements. However, they differ in the type of data collected and how the data are collected. Common types of control charts [bib#527] are:

- Individuals and Moving Range Chart (I-MR Chart or X-MR Chart): *continuous data, one data point collected at each point in time*

- Xbar and Range Chart (Xbar-R Chart*): continuous data, data collected in groups of between two and 10 (at least 2, but less than 10) observations*

- Xbar and Standard Deviation Chart (Xbar-S Chart*): continuous data, data collected in groups of at least 10 observations*

- *c*-Chart: *discrete data, number of defects per unit, number of samples of each sampling period is essentially the same*

- *u*-Chart: *discrete data, number of defects per unit, number of samples of each sampling period may vary significantly*

- *np*-Chart*: discrete data, whether the unit has at least one defect (whether unit is defective or not, unit is pass/fail), constant sampling size.*

- *p*-Chart: *discrete data, whether the unit has at least one defect (whether unit is defective or not, unit is pass/fail), sampling size is not constant*

There are many software packages designed specifically for control charts and SQC/SPC. Two of them are Infinity QS [bib#528] and PQ Systems [bib#529]. Excel is also able to produce control charts and ASQ provides a Control Chart Template, Excel [bib#530]. Add-in options for Excel to make control charts are also available from QI Macros [bib#531].

Additional interesting resources which discuss control charts in relation to healthcare organizations are:

- Statistical Process Control: Possible Uses to Monitor and Evaluate Patient-Centered Medical Home Models [bib#532]
- Application of statistical process control in healthcare improvement: systematic review [bib#533]

- Statistical process control as a tool for research and health care improvement [bib#534]

- Statistical Process Control [bib#535]

- Control Chart [bib#536]

- Statistical Process Control for Health Care [bib#537]

L3-T4. Histogram

The histogram [bib#538] is a common tool to display frequency (counts) in different categories both within and outside of QI programs. The histogram shows the distribution of data; for example, the distribution (frequency, count) of patients/customers arriving at an Emergency Room by day of the week. Most spreadsheet software such as Excel includes [bib#539] the histogram as a chart option. ASQ provides a quality-related histogram Excel template [bib#540]. ASQ states [bib#541] that the histogram is a:

 "*common graphical tool used to portray and visualize the distribution of a set of data ... It shows the form of the distribution by establishing the frequency of the data within a certain range. The histogram is constructed by taking the difference between the minimum and maximum observations and dividing it into evenly spaced intervals. Then, the number of observations in each interval is counted and the frequency is plotted as the height of a bar on the graph. The histogram is, in essence, a simplified view of the distribution that generated the plotted data.*"

ASQ also provides a description of how to do a histogram analysis [bib#542] and that such an analysis using a histogram can be useful to see whether a process change has occurred from one time period to another or determine whether the outputs of two or more processes are different. The ASQ Typical Histogram Shapes and What They Mean [bib#543] website discusses different types of histograms. The eight histogram shapes discussed at this site are:

- Normal
- Skewed
- Double-peaked or bimodal
- Plateau
- Edge peak
- Comb
- Truncated or heart-cut
- Dog food

L3 Topic 5 (T5). What are the Pareto Chart, Scatter Diagram, and Stratification tools for quality in healthcare organizations?

As mentioned in Topic 3, there are tools and methods commonly found in quality improvement (QI) work with which any QI professional should be familiar. They are: 1) cause-and-effect diagram, 2) check sheet, 3) control charts, 4) histogram, 5) pareto chart, 6) scatter diagram, and 7) stratification. The first four (cause-and-effect diagram, check sheet, control charts, histogram) were discussed in Topic 3 and Topic 4.

This section addresses:

- Pareto Chart
- Scatter Diagram
- Stratification

L3-T5. Pareto Chart

A Pareto chart can be considered a histogram (bar chart) to display counts (frequencies) arranged in descending order combined with a line graph to represent percentages. The category with the largest count is the first bar. The categories/bars and then placed next to each other in descending order in terms of count (frequency). The line graph placed above each bar represents the percentage each category (each bar) adds to the total percentage. The American Society for Quality (ASQ) states that [bib#544] a:

> "*Pareto chart is a bar graph. The lengths of the bars represent frequency or cost (time or money), and are arranged with longest bars on the left and the shortest to the right. In this way the chart visually depicts which situations are more significant*".

The utility of a Pareto chart is based in the Pareto Principle which is: 80 percent of a situation/problem is the result of 20 percent of the causes. A pareto chart helps a quality improvement team easily and visually identify the causes/factors which most affect the existence of a situation/problem.

*****

Video [bib#545]*: The video for Topic 5 – **Pareto Chart** –- is a YouTube video produced by the Western Region Public Health Training Center. This video discusses the relationship of a Pareto chart to a quality improvement program.   The link for the video is:*
https://www.youtube.com/watch?v=pLWBG_CZ4ZY

*****

Most spreadsheet software such as Excel includes the pareto chart as a chart option [bib#546]. ASQ provides a quality-related Pareto chart Excel template [bib#547].

Additional interesting resources on the topic are:

- When to Use a Pareto Chart [bib#548]

- [What is a Pareto Chart?](#) [bib#549]
- [Purpose of a Pareto Chart](#) [bib#550]
- [Pareto Charts](#) [bib#551]
- [Pareto Diagram](#) [bib#552]

L3-T5.   Scatter Diagram

A [scatter diagram](#) [bib#553] (also known as a scatter plot) is a common tool to display the relationship between two variables on one graph both within and outside of Quality Improvement (QI) programs. For example, the scatter diagram can show the relationship between height and weight. A person's height and weight are recorded and plotted: the x-axis can be height and the y-axis can be weight. A person whose height is 5' 0" and weight is 100 pounds would be represented by a point with the value (5,100); that is, x=5 and y=100. [ASQ states that](#) [bib#554] the scatter diagram:

> *"graphs pairs of numerical data, with one variable on each axis, to look for a relationship between them. If the variables are correlated, the points will fall along a line or curve. The better the correlation, the tighter the points will hug the line"*.

Most spreadsheet software such as Excel [includes the scatter diagram](#) [bib#555] as a chart option. ASQ provides a quality-related [scatter diagram Excel template](#) [bib#556].

Additional interesting resources on the topic are:

- [Scatter Plot](#) [bib#557]
- [Scatter Diagram, MathWorld](#) [bib#558]

L3-T5.   Stratification

Stratification, sometimes called [stratified sampling](#) [bib#559], is [defined by ASQ](#) [bib#560] as:

"a technique used in combination with other data analysis tools. When data from a variety of sources or categories have been lumped together, the meaning of the data can be impossible to see. This technique separates the data so that patterns can be seen."

For example, if a healthcare organization wanted to determine if patient/customer satisfaction differed by department or health care delivered, instead of asking all patients/customers leaving the healthcare organization their thoughts, the organization could organize the data collection by department. The healthcare organization could ensure that, for example, 10 patients/customers from each department were asked the question. Organizing the data collection by department is stratification. ASQ provides an Excel template illustrating stratification [bib#561].

Additional resources of interest on this topic are:

- Stratification Leads to Specialized Improvements [bib#562]
- Stratification [bib#563]

L3 Discussion Question: Quality Data Collection Challenges in Healthcare Organizations

What do you think are the greatest challenges in collecting the data from the identified quality measures for quality improvement in healthcare organizations? For example, do you think it is identifying the relevant quality measures? Or is it collecting the data itself such as any needed from patient/customer surveys?

L3 Quiz and "Create Your Own Healthcare Organization Quality Improvement Program"

L3 Quiz

Question 1

_____ Data represent categories (discrete, categorical data) of a measure which can be assigned a number (usually an integer like 1, 2, ...) which has meaning in terms of the order.

The answer to this question is found in Topic 1 and in the Lesson Three Quiz Answer Key at the end of the Lesson Three Quiz

Question 2

"Data which represent a measurement (continuous data) of a measure and has a true zero; there is a true absence of the measure" is the definition of:

A. Interval Data
B. Ordinal Data
C. Ratio Data
D. Nominal Data

The answer to this question is found in Topic 1 and in the Lesson Three Quiz Answer Key at the end of the Lesson Three Quiz

Question 3

Data documentation *"describes the contents, structure, and layout of a data collection ... information intended to be complete and self-explanatory for each variable in a data file"*.

A. True
B. False

The answer to this question is found in Topic 1 and in the Lesson Three Quiz Answer Key at the end of the Lesson Three Quiz

Question 4

Which of the following is **not** an example of a qualitative research design?

A. Phenomenology
B. Grounded Theory
C. Crosstabs Chi-Square

The answer to this question is found in Topic 2 and in the Lesson Three Quiz Answer Key at the end of the Lesson Three Quiz

Question 5

Random sampling is when samples are chosen randomly with each unit in the population having an equal chance of being selected for the sample.

A. True
B. False

The answer to this question is found in Topic 2 and in the Lesson Three Quiz Answer Key at the end of the Lesson Three Quiz

Question 6

Design of Experiments (DOE) is a strategy that can collect data and draw conclusions on more than one factor at a time.

A. True
B. False

The answer to this question is found in Topic 2 and in the Lesson Three Quiz Answer Key at the end of the Lesson Three Quiz

Question 7

The seven quality tools considered basic for quality improvement are: 1) cause-and-effect diagram, 2) check sheet, 3) control charts, 4) histogram, 5) Pareto chart, 6) scatter diagram, and 7) stratification.

A. True
B. False

The answer to this question is found in Topic 3 and in the Lesson Three Quiz Answer Key at the end of the Lesson Three Quiz

Question 8

A cause-and-effect diagram is also known as the Ishikawa chart or fishbone chart. The purpose of the diagram is to visually represent the possible causes for a quality problem situation (effect) which is the focus of quality improvement (QI).

A. True

B. False

The answer to this question is found in Topic 3 and in the Lesson Three Quiz Answer Key at the end of the Lesson Three Quiz

Question 9

The check sheet is a data collection tool to track *"effects"* – to track when, where, etc a specific quality problem occurs.

A. True

B. False

The answer to this question is found in Topic 3 and in the Lesson Three Quiz Answer Key at the end of the Lesson Three Quiz

Question 10

The American Society for Quality (ASQ) defines a control chart as "*a graph used to study how a process changes over time. Data are plotted in time order ... a central line for the average, an upper line for the upper control limit and a lower line for the lower control limit. These lines are determined from historical data. By comparing current data to these lines, you can draw conclusions about whether the process variation is consistent (in control) or is unpredictable (out of control, affected by special causes of variation)*".

A. True

B. False

The answer to this question is found in Topic 4 and in the Lesson Three Quiz Answer Key at the end of the Lesson Three Quiz

Question 11

For those people who consider there to be a difference between Statistical Quality Control (SQC) and Statistical Process Control (SPC), they often state that "*Statistical quality control (SQC) is the application of ... statistical and analytical tools ... to monitor process outputs (dependent variables). Statistical process control (SPC) is the application of the same ... tools to control process inputs (independent variables)*".

A. True

B. False

The answer to this question is found in Topic 4 and in the Lesson Three Quiz Answer Key at the end of the Lesson Three Quiz

Question 12

ASQ states that the histogram is a "*common graphical tool used to portray and visualize the distribution of a set of data ... It shows the form of the distribution by establishing the frequency of the data within a certain range. The histogram is constructed by taking the difference between the minimum and maximum observations and dividing it into evenly spaced intervals. Then, the number of observations in each interval is counted and the frequency is plotted as the height of a bar on the graph. The histogram is, in essence, a simplified view of the distribution that generated the plotted data.*"

A. True

B. False

The answer to this question is found in Topic 4 and in the Lesson Three Quiz Answer Key at the end of the Lesson Three Quiz

Question 13

American Society for Quality (ASQ) states that a "*Pareto chart is a bar graph. The lengths of the bars represent frequency or cost (time or money),* and are arranged with longest bars on the left and the shortest to the right. In this way the chart visually depicts which situations are more significant".

A. True
B. False

The answer to this question is found in Topic 5 and in the Lesson Three Quiz Answer Key at the end of the Lesson Three Quiz.

Question 14

ASQ states that the scatter diagram "*graphs pairs of numerical data, with one variable on each axis, to look for a relationship between them. If the variables are correlated, the points will fall along a line or curve. The better the correlation, the tighter the points will hug the line*".

A. True
B. False

The answer to this question is found in Topic 5 and in the Lesson Three Quiz Answer Key at the end of the Lesson Three Quiz.

Question 15

ASQ states that stratification is "*a technique used in combination with other data analysis tools. When data from a variety of sources or categories have been lumped together, the meaning of the data can be impossible to see. This technique separates the data so that patterns can be seen.*"

A. True
B. False

The answer to this question is found in Topic 5 and in the Lesson Three Quiz Answer Key at the end of the Lesson Three Quiz.

L3 Quiz Answer Key

Q1 = Ordinal; Q2 = C; Q3 = A; Q4 = C; Q5 = A; Q6 = A; Q7 = A; Q8 = A; Q9 = A; Q10 = A; Q11 = A; Q12 = A; Q13 = A; Q14 = A; Q15 = A

L3 "Create Your Own Healthcare Organization Quality Improvement Program"

In Lesson Four, you will *Design a Healthcare Organization Quality Improvement Program*. This competency development task requires that you synthesize content to create your own quality improvement program within a healthcare organization the way you would have things run in the best of all worlds. The type of healthcare organization is your choice (e.g., physical therapy office, dentist office, pharmacy, hospital, doctor's office).

Your synthesized information will be organized as an electronic spreadsheet. An example of a completed spreadsheet project is found in *Appendix B: Spreadsheet Example*. The spreadsheet is an artifact which you can circulate to colleagues or use for a talk or presentation event. Many people use Microsoft Excel for this purpose. However, there are many software options other than Excel. Some are available at no cost such as Calc [bib#198] which is part of LibreOffice [bib#199].

Eleven (11) content items and six (6) design items are suggested for the electronic spreadsheet task to develop competency. However, it is best not to wait until Lesson Four to begin to synthesize content to create your own quality improvement program within a healthcare organization. The earlier in your learning path that you begin this creation process, the better your own quality improvement program within a healthcare organization will be.

So in each lesson prior to Lesson Four, there will be an opportunity to begin to synthesize material – an opportunity to begin to create your own quality improvement program within a healthcare organization using material presented in that lesson. Of the eleven (11) suggested content items for the completed spreadsheet, three (3) are suggested for consideration in this lesson. Each is posted below and includes an expanded description as well as an example. They are:

Suggested Spreadsheet Content Item 9

A brief description of the type of data collected for your chosen quality measure (nominal, ordinal, interval, ratio).

There is no right or wrong answer to this question. It just has to be reasoned and make sense.

Example: The data on the quality measures collected with the Adult Hospital Survey (HCAHPS [bib#223]) are all ordinal. The answers to the questions are generally coded 1, 2, 3, and 4, where the lower the number the lower the quality. Answers coded 1 and 2 could be considered to be indicative of low quality.

Suggested Spreadsheet Content Item 10

A brief description as to how the data is collected for the quality measure.

There is no right or wrong answer to this question. It just has to be reasoned and make sense.

Example: The HCAPHS survey is sent to all patients discharged from HCAPHS within three days of discharge.

Suggested Spreadsheet Content Item 11

The display of some possible data for the chosen quality measure using a relevant tool available with the chosen spreadsheet package.
There is no right or wrong answer to this question. It just has to be reasoned and make sense.

Example: The dimensions/categories of the HCAPIIS survey which relate to person-centeredness are:

- *Communication with doctors*

- *Communication with nurses*
- *Responsiveness of hospital staff*
- *Communication about medicines*
- *Discharge information*

For the purposes of this project, the relevant data for each dimension/category is the number of patient/customers whose response was either a 1 or a 2. Of 100 surveyed patients/customers, for the purposes of this project, the number who gave a 1 or a 2 to:

- Communication with doctors = 45
- Communication with nurses = 52
- Responsiveness of hospital staff = 31
- Communication about medicines = 21
- Discharge information = 65

A Pareto chart will be used to display and analyze this information.

L3 Trivia Question and Virtual Field Trip

L3 Trivia Question

Almost everyone loves a trivia question – a question about a little known, but interesting, fun fact. Each lesson has one trivia question. The answer is in the Lesson Three Trivia Question Answer section.

Question:

Medicinal plants [bib#564] have always played a role in health care delivery. For this reason, some people go to great lengths to ensure that certain plant-types continue to exist. One of the most well-known – and extraordinary – examples of this are the people of the Russian Institute of Plant Industry in St.

Petersburg (then known as Leningrad). It was established in 1921 and the first head of the Institute was Nikolai Ivanovich Vavilov [bib#565].

At the start of the Siege of Leningrad [bib#566] (1941 - 1944), the Institute had accumulated seeds [bib#567] from "*187,000 varieties of plants, of which about 40,000 were food crops*". The Institute staff went to extraordinary lengths to protect the collection during the Siege and ensure the collection's survival. Many of the staff starved to death rather than eat any of the seeds.

The Institute still exists [bib#568] (known now as the Vavilov Institute of Plant Industry) and continues its work, but there is now also a global seed repository which serves as a backup for the Institute's repository of seeds. *What is the name of this backup repository and where is it located?*

L3 Trivia Question Answer

The answer to the Lesson Three trivia question is:

Global Seed Vault in Svalbard, Norway

The Seed Vault has a capacity of 2.5 billion seeds with a plan to store 500 seeds of each of 4.5 million different types of seeds/crops. Currently, the Vault holds more than 968,000 samples from almost every country in the world making it one of the most diverse collections of food crop seeds in the world. The plan is that the 1700 current seed repositories send duplicates of their seed collections to the Seed Vault as a backup.

For more information, please see:

- Facts About the Global Seed Vault [bib#569]
- Svalbard Global Seed Vault [bib#570]
- Wikipedia, Global Seed Vault [bib#571]

L3 Virtual Field Trip

Everyone loves a road trip/field trip so each lesson includes a "*virtual field trip*" to the often hidden places of interest on the web.

Lesson Three's virtual field trip is to the United States Botanic Garden [bib#572] (USBG) which is:

"*a living plant museum that informs visitors about the importance, and often irreplaceable value, of plants to the well-being of humans and to earth's fragile ecosystems. More than 200 years ago, George Washington had a vision for the capital city of the United States that included a botanic garden that would demonstrate and promote the importance of plants to the young nation. Established by the U.S. Congress in 1820, the U.S. Botanic Garden is one of the oldest botanic gardens in North America ... The U.S. Botanic Garden is dedicated to demonstrating the aesthetic, cultural, economic, therapeutic and ecological importance of plants to the well-being of humankind.*"

****

> **Video** [bib#573]: *The video for the Lesson Three Virtual Field Trip – **United States Botanic Garden** – is a YouTube video produced by the U.S. Capitol. It is an overview and tour of the United States Botanic Garden. The link for the video is:* https://www.youtube.com/watch?v=HpSbhezAVTU

*****

Lesson Four (L4): Design a Healthcare Organization Quality Improvement Program

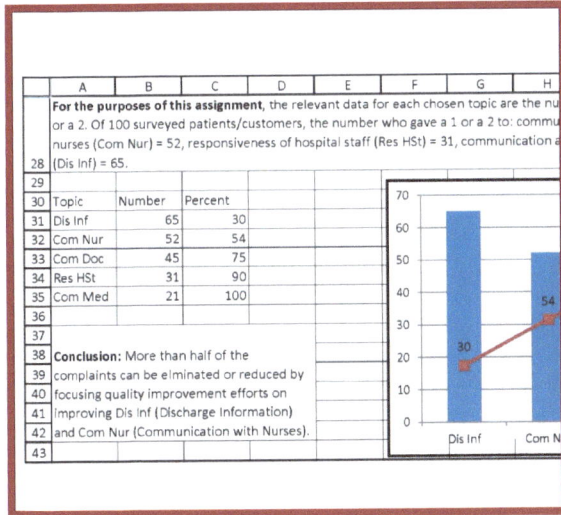

	A	B	C	D	E	F	G	H
	For the purposes of this assignment, the relevant data for each chosen topic are the nu							
	or a 2. Of 100 surveyed patients/customers, the number who gave a 1 or a 2 to: commu							
	nurses (Com Nur) = 52, responsiveness of hospital staff (Res HSt) = 31, communication a							
28	(Dis Inf) = 65.							
29								
30	Topic	Number	Percent					
31	Dis Inf	65	30					
32	Com Nur	52	54					
33	Com Doc	45	75					
34	Res HSt	31	90					
35	Com Med	21	100					
36								
37								
38	**Conclusion:** More than half of the							
39	complaints can be elminated or reduced by							
40	focusing quality improvement efforts on							
41	Improving Dis Inf (Discharge Information)							
42	and Com Nur (Communication with Nurses).							
43								

L4 Competency Objectives

This lesson is a synthesis of the course material to design a quality improvement program in a healthcare organization the way you would have things run in the best of all worlds. The competency objectives are:

- Synthesize content to create a quality improvement program for a healthcare organization

- Generate an effective quality improvement spreadsheet suitable for discussion, presentation, and printing.

L4 Content and Discussion

This lesson is a synthesis of the content material to design and present a quality improvement program in a healthcare organization the way you would have things run in the best of all worlds. The purpose of this lesson is to help you improve your skills in presenting your point of view and arguing for your view of the best quality improvement program in a healthcare organization

There are two topic sections, a discussion question, two self-evaluations, one electronic spreadsheet file creation, a trivia question, and a field trip. The electronic spreadsheet file is an artifact of the book's learning path which you can circulate to colleagues or use for a talk or presentation event. The lesson should take 4 - 6 hours of work to successfully complete. There are also videos which provide supplemental content which can help you better define your personal learning path. There are many wonderful videos in the public domain which are relevant to the topics in this book.

In constructing your electronic spreadsheet, you are going to do so from the perspective of the chief healthcare administrator for your organization. Healthcare administration encompasses responsibility for all aspects of a healthcare organization. The focus is both internal to the organization and external to the organization to maximize the efficient and effective operation of the organization as a whole and its survival both short-term and long term. Healthcare administrators make decisions about the direction and operation of the healthcare organization. The role of the healthcare administrator is more strategic than tactical.

The two topics for Lesson Four are:

1. Suggested content for the spreadsheet
2. Suggested format for the spreadsheet

L4 Topic 1 (T1). Suggested content for the spreadsheet

The spreadsheet project suggests that you synthesize material to design a quality improvement program in a healthcare organization the way you would have things run in the best of all worlds. The spreadsheet file is an artifact of the book's learning path which you can circulate to colleagues or use for a talk or presentation event. An example of a completed spreadsheet project is found in *Appendix B: Spreadsheet Example*.

In constructing your spreadsheet, you are going to do so from the perspective of the chief healthcare administrator for your organization. You are describing your organization's quality improvement program to an audience.

Healthcare administration encompasses responsibility for all aspects of a healthcare organization. The focus is both internal to the organization and external to the organization to maximize the efficient and effective operation of the organization as a whole and its survival both short-term and long term. Healthcare administrators make decisions about the direction and operation of the healthcare organization. The role of the healthcare administrator is more strategic than tactical.

The eleven (11) suggested spreadsheet content items were specified in the first three lessons. You can certainly add more content to your spreadsheet than the suggested eleven (11) content items – or less. Each one of the suggested eleven items is listed (once again) below with an example and the suggested self-evaluation rubric (evaluation criterion).

In the *Lesson Four Self-Evaluations* section is a "*quiz*" entitled *Synthesize Content Self-Evaluation*. This quiz is a self-evaluation as to whether you have accomplished the synthesis of content described here. Not surprising, it is an eleven (11) question quiz asking whether you have developed the eleven suggested spreadsheet content items.

Suggested Spreadsheet Content Item 1: The name of your healthcare organization in which you will design your quality improvement program.

- Example: Charles Harbor General Hospital (CHGH)

- *Evaluation Rubric: The name should be original and give some sense to healthcare consumers as to the healthcare products found in the organization. The Charles River runs through Boston and Cambridge and into the Boston Harbor. Names are important. They are part of public relations (PR) for the organization.*

Suggested Spreadsheet Content Item 2: A brief description of your healthcare organization; a description of what your healthcare organization does.

- Example: Charles Harbor General Hospital (CHGH) is a private, non-profit, general hospital in Massachusetts. It has an emergency room and a full range of clinical specialties (e.g., internal medicine, general surgery, oncology, cardiology, infectious disease, pediatrics).

- *Evaluation Rubric: The description should be a few sentences which concisely and clearly summarize for healthcare consumers the type of healthcare organization, its location, and its product. In the description give the scope of the organization's effort. Again, you can think of this as PR for the organization.*

Suggested Spreadsheet Content Item 3: A brief description of which quality improvement framework/model you use in your healthcare organization and why. You can use one discussed in the book (e.g., Lean, Six Sigma) or choose another.

- Example: CHGH uses Lean Six Sigma because of the focus on first using the Lean strategy to eliminate waste (make the processes more cost effective) and then using Six Sigma to reduce errors/defects in the Lean streamlined processes by either improving them or replacing them. It makes little sense to focus on processes before they have been streamlined.

- *Evaluation Rubric: Any position on a quality improvement framework is acceptable. It just has to make sense in terms of its relationship to the healthcare organization*

Suggested Spreadsheet Content Item 4: Choose and display one of the six health care/healthcare organization quality domains on which to focus your quality improvement program. Include a brief description why you chose that domain.

- Example: CHGH focuses the quality improvement program on person-centeredness. CHGH considers patient/customer satisfaction to be essential to quality at CHGH. A key to patient/customer satisfaction is ensuring that all organizational processes are person-centered.

- *Evaluation Rubric: The list of quality domains, listed as the Six Dimensions of Health Care Quality, are: 1) Safety; 2) Effectiveness; 3) Person-Centeredness; 4) Accessibility, Timeliness, Affordability; 5) Efficiency; and 6) Equity. Although they are listed as dimensions/domains of Health Care Quality, they can also be considered dimensions/domains of Healthcare Organization Quality. Any one choice from the six quality domains is acceptable. It just has to make sense in terms of its relationship to the healthcare organization*

Suggested Spreadsheet Content Item 5: A brief outline of the key components of your quality improvement program in your chosen quality domain.

- Example: CHGH's person-centeredness quality improvement program is aimed at continuously improving the quality of person-centeredness in all aspects of CHGH functioning. To that purpose the quality improvement program is coordinated by the Office of Quality Improvement which actively: 1) Views CHGH as a system within which is a sub-system of processes related to ensuring person-centeredness quality. The person-centeredness quality system cuts across all departments and units at CHGH; 2) Understands and respects the CHGH patient/customer expectations/requirements of person-centeredness quality when interacting with CHGH; 3)Ensures that all CHGH personnel work as a team to improve person-centeredness quality; and 4)Collects and analyzes both qualitative and quantitative data to track person-centeredness quality across all of CHGH.

- *Evaluation Rubric: HRSA states that all successful QI programs in healthcare organizations include a focus on: 1) The operation of the healthcare organization as a system and sub-systems comprised of resources/inputs (e.g., health care delivery professionals), activities/processes (e.g., health care delivery actions), and outputs/outcomes (e.g., change in patient/customer health status); 2) Patient/customer exceptions/requirements of the healthcare organization as a whole and, specifically, the health care delivered; 3) The need for everyone in the healthcare organization to work as a team with a common goal of QI; and 4) Collecting and analyzing both qualitative and quantitative data to track quality. Any position on a quality improvement framework is acceptable. It just has to make sense in terms of its relationship to the healthcare organization*

Suggested Spreadsheet Content Item 6: A list of one or more quality improvement professional organizations to which you might belong. It could be one listed in the lesson or another one. Include a brief description of your reasoning for the choice.

- Example: American Society for Quality (ASQ) because of the large array of quality resources available to members.

- *Evaluation Rubric: Any position on a quality improvement framework is acceptable. It just has to make sense in terms of its relationship to the healthcare organization*

Suggested Spreadsheet Content Item 7: Which of the three types of measures (structural, procedural, or outcome) is the focus of your quality improvement program and why?

- Example: Outcome measures are the focus. For person-centeredness quality, the outcome, the perception of person-centeredness by patients/customers is the key measure. It matters little how hard CHGH tries - what the structure and process are - if the outcome from the perspective of the patient/customer is not of high quality.

- *Evaluation Rubric: Any position on a quality improvement framework is acceptable. It just has to make sense in terms of its relationship to the healthcare organization*

Suggested Spreadsheet Content Item 8: A list at least one measure that you use in your quality improvement program and a brief description why the measure was chosen.

- Example: The primary measure used by CHGH to measure patient/customer satisfaction to increase the quality of person-centeredness is the Adult Hospital Survey (HCAHPS) which "*asks people 18 and older about their experiences with medical, surgical, or obstetric care provided in an inpatient setting*". This was chosen because it is used by more than 4000 hospitals in the United States which means it is reliable and valid and allows for benchmarking. Personnel from the Office of Quality Improvement also monitor reviews on such sites as Yelp and respond as necessary. Personnel also routinely visit patient/customer waiting areas and informally ask some patients/customers on a daily basis to provide informal feedback. The HCAHPS Survey contains 21 patient perspectives on care and patient rating items that encompass nine key topics: communication with doctors, communication with nurses, responsiveness of hospital staff, pain management, communication about medicines, discharge information, cleanliness of the hospital environment, quietness of the hospital environment, and transition of care. The survey also includes four screener questions and seven demographic items, which are used for adjusting the mix of patients across hospitals and for analytical purposes. The survey is 32 questions in length. There are four approved modes of administration for the CAHPS Hospital Survey: 1) Mail Only; 2) Telephone Only; 3) Mixed (mail followed by telephone); and 4) Active Interactive Voice Response (IVR). From https://www.hcahpsonline.org/

- *Evaluation Rubric: Any position on a quality improvement framework is acceptable. It just has to make sense in terms of its relationship to the healthcare organization*

<u>Suggested Spreadsheet Content Item 9:</u> Briefly describe the type of data collected for your chosen quality measure (nominal, ordinal, interval, ratio).

- <u>Example:</u> The data on the quality measures collected with the HCAPHS survey are all ordinal. The survey can be found at *https://www.hcahpsonline.org/en/survey-instruments/* and the answers to the questions are generally coded 1, 2, 3, and 4, where the lower the number the lower the quality. Answers coded 1 and 2 could be considered to be indicative of low quality.

- *Evaluation Rubric: Any position on a quality improvement framework is acceptable. It just has to make sense in terms of its relationship to the healthcare organization*

<u>Suggested Spreadsheet Content Item 10:</u> Briefly describe how the data is collected for the quality measure.

- <u>Example:</u> The HCAPHS survey is sent to all patients discharged from HCAPHS within three days of discharge

- *Evaluation Rubric: Any position on a quality improvement framework is acceptable. It just has to make sense in terms of its relationship to the healthcare organization*

<u>Suggested Spreadsheet Content Item 11:</u> Create some possible data for your chosen quality measure and display it using a relevant tool available with your chosen spreadsheet package.

- <u>Example:</u> The dimensions/categories of the HCAPHS survey which relate to person-centeredness are: *communication with doctors, communication with nurses, responsiveness of hospital staff, communication about medicines, and discharge information.* For the purposes of this assignment, the relevant data for each dimension/category is the number of patient/customers whose response was either a 1 or a 2. Of 100 surveyed patients/customers, the number who gave a 1 or a 2 to: communication with doctors = 45, communication with nurses = 52, responsiveness of hospital staff = 31, communication about medicines = 21, and discharge information = 65. A Pareto Chart will be used to display and analyze this information.

- *Evaluation Rubric: Any position on a quality improvement framework is acceptable. It just has to make sense in terms of its relationship to the healthcare organization*

It is suggested that this synthesized information should be organized as an electronic spreadsheet. The next section discusses the creation of the electronic spreadsheet file. Many people use Microsoft Excel for this purpose. However, there are many software options other than Excel. Some are available at no cost such as Calc [bib#198] which is part of LibreOffice [bib#199].

*****

> *Video* [bib#574]: *The video for Topic 1 – LibreOffice-Calc, OpenOffice-Calc, Excel Tutorial - A first Look – is a YouTube video produced by TheFrugalComputerGuy. The video provides a brief introduction to the LibreOffice Calc spreadsheet software. The link for the video is:*
> https://www.youtube.com/watch?v=HdOLxR_NlrQ

*****

L4 Topic 2 (T2). Suggested format for the spreadsheet

The spreadsheet project suggests that you synthesize material to design a quality improvement program in a healthcare organization the way you would have things run in the best of all worlds. The suggested synthesis items were described in Topic 1 of Lesson Four. An example of a completed spreadsheet is found in *Appendix B: Spreadsheet Example*.

The electronic spreadsheet file is an artifact which you can circulate to colleagues or use for a talk or presentation event. In constructing your spreadsheet, it is suggested that you do so from the perspective of the chief healthcare administrator for your organization. You are describing your healthcare organization quality improvement program to an audience.

The basic process for generating an effective electronic spreadsheet file is:

1. Choose the spreadsheet software to use
2. Add the content to the spreadsheet
3. Iterate to improve

In the ***Lesson Four Self-Evaluations*** section of this book is a quiz entitled ***Generate an Effective Spreadsheet Self-Evaluation***. This quiz is a self-evaluation as to whether you have generated an effective electronic spreadsheet. It is a six (6) question quiz asking whether you have incorporated the 6 suggested format/design characteristics into your spreadsheet. These six are only suggestions. The spreadsheet format/design is yours to choose. The six suggested characteristics are:

Suggested Format/Design Characteristic 1: The electronic spreadsheet is between 1 and 3 pages; landscape orientation.

Suggested Format/Design Characteristic 2: There is a page number on each page of the spreadsheet.

Suggested Format/Design Characteristic 3: There is an adequate margin on each side of the page.

Suggested Format/Design Characteristic 4: One font-type is used for the entire spreadsheet. The chosen font-type is easily readable and not distracting from the content.

Suggested Format/Design Characteristic 5: There is a title for the spreadsheet at the top of the first page which is less than 15 words and provides the reader with a clear understanding of the spreadsheet's focus.

Suggested Format/Design Characteristic 6: The author of the spreadsheet is stated on the first page.

*****

Video [bib#575]: *The first video for Topic 2 –* **Libre Office - Calc, Open Office - Calc, Excel Tutorial - Charts Data Series** *– is a YouTube video produced by TheFrugalComputerGuy. The video provides information on how to develop charts in Calc. The link for the video is:*
https://www.youtube.com/watch?v=MEUuwq7FS7k

*****

*****

Video [bib#576]: *The second video for Topic 2 –* **20 Principles for Good Spreadsheet Practice** *– is a YouTube video produced by Microsoft UK. It is an overview of twenty principles to following when developing and using spreadsheet software. The link for the video is:*
https://www.youtube.com/watch?v=UK_YpZBB02Y

*****

L4 Self-Evaluations

At this point, you should have *Designed a Healthcare Organization Quality Improvement Program* – if you have chosen to do so – within a healthcare organization the way you would have things run in the best of all worlds. The type of healthcare organization is your choice (e.g., physical therapy office, dentist office, pharmacy, hospital, doctor's office).

It is suggested that this design be organized as an electronic spreadsheet file according to the seventeen (17) items/criteria suggested earlier. As such, the last two (and in some ways the most important) competency development tasks arc your personal evaluation of the electronic spreadsheet you developed.

The quality of a spreadsheet for presentation is usually judged on two major factors: 1) whether the spreadsheet content is sufficient for its intended purpose, and 2) whether the spreadsheet appearance is such that the content can be grasped relatively easily. Most spreadsheets are produced for a specific purpose (e.g., a conference, a meeting, an analysis) and the sufficiency of the content is related to its purpose. The quality of a spreadsheet for presentation (content presentation and format) is usually evaluated relative to its intended purpose.

For the purposes of this suggested competency development task, the evaluation criteria are the seventeen (17) suggested items/criteria discussed earlier. Clearly, you can ignore them and establish your own different criteria.

An example of a spreadsheet with the seventeen (17) suggested items/criteria items – eleven (11) suggested content items and the six (6) suggested template/design characteristics – is found in *Appendix B: Spreadsheet Example*.

Your personal evaluation of your electronic spreadsheet – for the purposes of this suggested competency development task – is divided into two self-evaluations:

1. Synthesize Content Self-Evaluation
2. Generate an Effective Electronic Spreadsheet Self-Evaluation

The questions for each of the two self-evaluations are shown below.

L4 Quiz: Synthesize Content Self-Evaluation

<u>Question 1</u>

Does the spreadsheet display a name for the healthcare organization in which the quality improvement program is designed that is original and gives some sense to healthcare consumers as to the healthcare products found in the organization?.

O   Yes
O   No

This is your own personal self-evaluation of the synthesized material suggested for the electronic spreadsheet.

Question 2

Does the spreadsheet display a brief description of the healthcare organization (a description of what the healthcare organization does) which concisely and clearly summarizes for healthcare consumers the type of healthcare organization, its location, and its products in a few sentences?

O   Yes
O   No

This is your own personal self-evaluation of the synthesized material suggested for the electronic spreadsheet.

Question 3

Does the spreadsheet briefly describe which quality improvement framework/model is used in the healthcare organization and why? It can be one discussed in the course (e.g., Lean, Six Sigma) or another.

O   Yes
O   No

This is your own personal self-evaluation of the synthesized material suggested for the electronic spreadsheet.

Question 4

Does the spreadsheet display a choice of one of the six health care/healthcare organization quality domains on which the quality improvement program is focused and briefly describe why that domain was chosen?

O   Yes
O   No

This is your own personal self-evaluation of the synthesized material suggested for the electronic spreadsheet.

Question 5

Does the spreadsheet briefly outline the key components of the quality improvement program in the chosen quality domain?

O   Yes
O   No

This is your own personal self-evaluation of the synthesized material suggested for the electronic spreadsheet.

Question 6

Does the spreadsheet list one or more quality improvement professional organizations to which the CEO could belong? It could be one listed in the lesson or another one. Is the reasoning for the choice briefly described?

O   Yes
O   No

This is your own personal self-evaluation of the synthesized material suggested for the electronic spreadsheet.

Question 7

Does the spreadsheet list which of the three types of measures (structural, procedural, or outcome) is the focus of the quality improvement program and why?

O   Yes
O   No

This is your own personal self-evaluation of the synthesized material suggested for the electronic spreadsheet.

Question 8

Does the spreadsheet list at least one measure that was used in the quality improvement program and describe why the measure was chosen?

O   Yes

O   No

This is your own personal self-evaluation of the synthesized material suggested for the electronic spreadsheet.

Question 9

Does the spreadsheet display a brief description of the type of data collected for the chosen quality measure (nominal, ordinal, interval, ratio)?

O   Yes
O   No

This is your own personal self-evaluation of the synthesized material suggested for the electronic spreadsheet.

Question 10

Does the spreadsheet briefly describe how the data is collected for the quality measure? There is no right or wrong answer to this question. It just has to be reasoned and make sense.

O   Yes
O   No

This is your own personal self-evaluation of the synthesized material suggested for the electronic spreadsheet.

Question 11

Does the spreadsheet display some possible data for the chosen quality measure and display it using a relevant tool available with the chosen spreadsheet package?

O   Yes
O   No

This is your own personal self-evaluation of the synthesized material suggested for the electronic spreadsheet.

L4 Quiz: Generate an Effective Electronic Spreadsheet Self-Evaluation

Question 1

Is the electronic spreadsheet between 1 and 3 pages; landscape orientation?

O   Yes
O   No

This is your own personal self-evaluation of the synthesized material suggested for the electronic spreadsheet.

Question 2

Is there is a page number on each page of the spreadsheet?

O   Yes
O   No

This is your own personal self-evaluation of the synthesized material suggested for the electronic spreadsheet.

Question 3

Is there an adequate margin on each side of the page?

O   Yes
O   No

This is your own personal self-evaluation of the synthesized material suggested for the electronic spreadsheet.

Question 4

Is one font-type is used for the entire spreadsheet? Is the chosen font-type is easily readable and not distracting from the content?

O   Yes
O   No

This is your own personal self-evaluation of the synthesized material suggested for the electronic spreadsheet.

Question 5

Is there is a title for the spreadsheet at the top of the first page which is less than 15 words and provides the reader with a clear understanding of the spreadsheet's focus?

O   Yes
O   No

This is your own personal self-evaluation of the synthesized material suggested for the electronic spreadsheet.

Question 6

Is the name of the spreadsheet's author stated on the first page?

O   Yes
O   No

This is your own personal self-evaluation of the synthesized material suggested for the electronic spreadsheet.

L4 Discussion Question: Spreadsheet Generation

What, if anything, surprised you most about the process of producing an electronic spreadsheet? What, if anything, would you do differently the next time you produce an electronic spreadsheet? What did you find most interesting, challenging, fun, ...?

L4 Trivia Question and Virtual Field Trip

L4 Trivia Question

Almost everyone loves a trivia question – a question about a little known, but interesting, fun fact. Each lesson has one trivia question. The answer is in the Lesson Four Trivia Question Answer reading section.

Question:

The security and privacy of patient information is of critical importance. But healthcare is not the only industry concerned with the security/privacy of information. It is important in many industries and endeavors, not the least of which is war and on the battlefield. Clearly, on the battlefield, you want to communicate with your own troops, but not let enemy troops know what you are planning. During World War II, only one American battlefield code was not broken by enemy troops. *What was this code and what were some of the reasons it was not broken?*

L4 Trivia Question Answer

The answer to the Lesson Four trivia question is:

The Navajo Code communicated by soldiers known as Navajo Marine Code Talkers.

The Navajo Marine Code Talkers were approximately 500 U.S. Marines – primarily members of the Navajo nation – fluent in the Navajo language. The Marines communicated battlefield information in Navajo – an unwritten language with a complex grammar in which very few people were fluent. These battlefield communications were said to be in the Navajo Code.

For more information, please see:

* 1942: Navajo Code Talkers [bib#577]

- Codetalker [bib#578]
- Navajo Windtalkers [bib#579]

L4 Virtual Field Trip

Everyone loves a road trip/field trip so each lesson of the course includes a "*virtual field trip*" to the often hidden places of interest on the web.

Lesson Four's virtual field trip is to the National Cryptologic Museum [bib#580] in Ft. George G. Meade, Maryland. The Museum is the

"*National Security Agency's principal gateway to the public. It shares the Nation's, as well as NSA's, cryptologic legacy and place in world history ... the Museum houses thousands of artifacts that collectively serve to sustain the history of the cryptologic profession*".

Cryptology is the study of cryptography and cryptanalysis. It is the study of the best way to develop "secret codes" that are really secret and break "secret codes". It is essentially the study of ways to enable those whom you want to receive a communication to be able to do so while keeping the information away from those whom you do not want to be able to understand the communication.

Encryption is a form of cryptology. Medical information send electronically between health care delivery providers must be encrypted in order to keep patient information private; in order for those who have a right and a need to know to be able to view it, while anyone else cannot.

More information can be found at:

- Department of Health and Human Services (HHS): Encryption [bib#581]
- Encryption vs. Cryptography – What is the Difference [bib#582]
- Basic cryptology concepts [bib#583]

> *Video* [bib#584]: *The video for the Lesson Four Virtual Field Trip – **Decoding the National Cryptologic Museum** – is a YouTube video produced by the Smithsonian Magazine. The video is an overview of the National Cryptologic Museum.* The link for the video is:
> https://www.youtube.com/watch?v=pses-io-Obw

L4 Wrapping Up

Book content included an overview of quality and quality improvement programs, measures, and data in healthcare organizations. If you have completed all of the competency development tasks you should have a better understanding of quality and quality improvement programs, measures, and data in healthcare organizations. If you work within a healthcare organization you should now be better able to contribute to the efficient and effective operations of your organization. You should be better able to undertake and improve healthcare quality and quality improvement system responsibilities within your organization.

The overall competency goal of this book was that it enabled you to think more critically and more independently about quality improvement in healthcare organizations.

Specifically, upon successful completion of this book, you should now be able to:

1. Define quality and quality improvement in healthcare organizations.

2. Define quality and quality improvement measures in healthcare organizations.

3. Define the data collection and analysis methodologies for quality and quality improvement measures in healthcare organizations.

4. Synthesize content to create a quality improvement program for a healthcare organization.

5. Generate an effective quality improvement spreadsheet suitable for discussion, presentation and printing.

The hope embedded in this book is that having achieved these objectives, you do not just know more now that you have read this book, but that you now think more critically and more independently about healthcare organization quality and quality improvement programs in new and interesting ways.

So if a personal goal is to be the best healthcare administrator: Find excellent mentors in healthcare administration. Find excellent healthcare administration peers. Do more healthcare administration than anyone else (e.g., read more about healthcare administration than anyone else, do more healthcare administration tasks than anyone else). It is hoped that the extra resources in this book (e.g., external links) help you accomplish these three steps.

But wherever your learning path and journey take you, the hope embedded in this book is that your path and journey are as pleasant and interesting as many of those which can be found in the National Parks of the United States [bib#585]. Some truly spectacular paths can be found in Zion National Park [bib#586] in Utah.

*****

> *Video* [bib#587]*: The video for this Wrapping Up section –* ***Angel's Landing - Scariest Hike in America? Steep Drop Off*** *– is a YouTube video produced by SoCal Attractions 360. The video is of a hike in Zion National Park. The link for the video is:* https://www.youtube.com/watch?v=jy6K0KoMrco

*****

L4 Discussion Question: Achievement of Personal Learning Goal

At the beginning of this book, you were asked to consider whether you had a personal learning goal for this learning path. If you did, was your goal achieved? Did you learn what you wanted to learn in this book? If not, what resources do you need to achieve your personal learning goal? What are your next steps?

Appendix A: Expanded Book Overview

The *About this Book* section at the beginning of this book gives a very brief overview of the book content and intent.   A longer, expanded overview is provided in this section. Appendix A is redundant with the information contained in the *About this Book* section. Appendix A is provided because some readers prefer a more detailed overview of the book than is provided in the *About this Book* section. This longer overview addresses five (5) topics organized as questions with answers. The questions/topics are:

1. What is a brief summary of this book?
2. How is the book content organized?
3. What are the competency objectives for readers?
4. What tasks facilitate development of competency objectives?
5. What is the educational philosophy of this book?

Appendix A Topic 1. What is a brief summary of this book?

Have you ever thought that healthcare quality could be improved – either where you get health care treatment or where you deliver health care? Have you ever thought that there should be a way for you to determine the relative quality of your healthcare choices? Have you found yourself thinking that there should be a way for you to provide your view and input on the quality of healthcare organization? Or do you work in a healthcare organization and find yourself thinking that there must be better ways to continuously and systematically improve the quality of your healthcare organization? If you have, this book is for you.

This book is an overview of quality and quality improvement programs, measures, and data in healthcare organizations. These topics are addressed from an evidence-based perspective. The evidence-based approach relies on data which are scientifically collected and analyzed using statistical techniques in the context of the literature. It is the foundational approach in modern health care quality improvement systems. The evidence-based approach is used as it informs and selects the best approaches (e.g., best treatment, best organizational structure, best quality measures). It is a central topic in this book.

This book is for those with a developing interest in the organizational operations, administration, and quality improvement in healthcare organizations and for those who have some expertise, but who wish an overview or refresher of these topics.

This book has an agenda or purpose aimed at aiding the reader. The book knows that you have your own specific personal goals regarding quality improvement in healthcare. The purpose of this book is to enable you to develop your own learning path to reach your learning goal regardless of what that goal happens to be. The intent of the book is to provide you with content and resources to pursue a personal learning path. That content extends past the reading of this text and will help you in your chosen work or study.

The format includes tons of resources (some would say encyclopedic) coupled with the Socratic Method and suggested competency development tasks. The Socratic Method promotes understanding of a topic by posing questions on that topic. An answer to the question requires a learner/reader to think critically and synthesize information. The overall competency goal for all readers of this book is that it enables each reader to think more critically and more independently about quality improvement in healthcare organizations.

The book is organized into four (4) lessons. Each lesson is organized around competency objectives, questions, readings, competency development tasks (e.g., quiz) to organize your thinking and cement your learning. It is a format which makes extensive use of the resources available on the internet. As such the book provides links to external sites to connect you to the larger "*real world*" of healthcare organizations to help you better build your own learning path. The links also serve as resources you can use after you complete this book. We want to emphasize that the list of resources provided for the reader is an important and valuable aspect of this book.

These links (more than 575) are directly accessible in the content in the e-book version. For the print version – and for reference in the e-book version – the full URL for each link in the book can be found at the corresponding in-text link number *(bib#)* in the section at the end of the book entitled *Bibliography: Associated URL/Link List.* The list includes data, management, and research links needed for healthcare administration, management, and operations related to quality improvement in a healthcare organization.

The competency development tasks in this book facilitate content mastery to help you organize your thinking. Such organized thought should help you determine the relationship between the book content, a personal learning path, and achievement of personal goals. Competency development tasks in this book are: discussion questions, quizzes, and the project. Again, this is a Socratic approach in that the book asks for your thinking on the topics.

The included project is intended to help you synthesize content material by designing a quality improvement program of your choice for a healthcare organization of your choice the way you would have things run in the best of all worlds. The design is communicated in electronic spreadsheet format. An example of a completed spreadsheet project is found in *Appendix B: Spreadsheet Example*. The spreadsheet is an artifact which you can circulate to colleagues or use as the basis for a talk or presentation event. The philosophy behind this project is that more learning occurs – and learning is more fun – if you can actually build/create something from the content and it is useful beyond the reading of this book.

And because everyone loves a road trip/field trip, there are also "*virtual field trips*" to the often hidden places of interest on the web. There are also trivia questions – just for fun – because everyone also loves little known, but interesting, fun facts.

This book is dense in the physics sense of the word. There is a lot of detail we have to introduce to get people on the playing field. There is no royal road to acquiring that depth of information. We have attempted to organize the information and to make it searchable. One needs to take a break every so often to absorb the material. This is one of the reasons why virtual field trips and trivia questions are provided. Historical and social context is important in healthcare. Many of the links, virtual field trips, and trivia questions provide this context.

This book follows the content of and can be used as an adjunct to the Coursera course: *Quality Improvement in Care Delivery in Healthcare*

Organizations found at https://www.coursera.org/learn/quality-improvement-in-healthcare-organizations. Should you prefer a learning experience which can result in an earned certificate or prefer a community of learners in the same course of study, consider enrolling in the Coursera course.

Appendix A Topic 2. How is the book content organized?

The book is organized into four (4) lessons. Each lesson should take 4 - 6 hours of work to successfully complete; total time commitment for the course of study defined by the book = 16 - 24 hours. The four lessons are:

1. Definition of Quality and Quality Improvement in Healthcare Organizations *(Primary Competency Development Task: Quiz)*

2. Quality and Quality Improvement Measures in Healthcare Organizations *(Primary Competency Development Task: Quiz)*

3. Data Collection and Analysis Methodologies for Quality and Quality Improvement Measures in Healthcare Organizations *(Primary Competency Development Task: Quiz)*

4. Design a Healthcare Organization Quality Improvement Program *(Primary Competency Development Task: Spreadsheet Project)*

For the spreadsheet project, you will need Excel software or its equivalent. There are many software options other than Excel. Some are available at no cost such as Calc [bib#198] which is part of LibreOffice [bib#199].

Each lesson is organized around readings, videos, and competency development tasks (i.e., discussion question, quiz, project) to organize your thinking and cement your learning with regard to the stated competency objective(s) for that lesson. The competency development tasks in this book facilitate content mastery to help you organize your thinking. Such organized thought should help you determine the relationship between the book content, a personal learning path, and achievement of personal goals. Again, this is a Socratic approach in that the book asks for your thinking on the topics.

- Again, readings are presented as a series of topic questions and answers – the Socratic Method – because it is a better and much more interesting way for a reader to master content.

- Some of the links in the book are to YouTube videos. Most of these videos are used to present interesting supplemental content to the readings and are not needed to complete the competency development tasks. Some link to a "*virtual field trip*" to the often hidden places of interest on the web.

- Each discussion question is a competency development task intended to help you consider important and interesting questions related to the readings content. The question is suitable for either discussion with others or your own personal thought and reflection. The purpose of the question is to facilitate critical, independent – as well as possibly new and interesting – ways to think about health care delivery in healthcare organizations.

- There are two types of quizzes in this book: content and self-evaluation. Each type of quiz is a competency development task. The first type contains multiple choice or fill-in-the-blank questions based in the designated readings. The purpose of each content quiz is to help you develop competency in the stated study objectives. There is nothing like being asked a question about a topic to help you learn and think critically about that topic. The answer key for each content quiz is at the end of the content quiz. The second type is a self-evaluation of the spreadsheet project content and format to ensure that you think critically about the spreadsheet project (e.g., if the reflects a synthesis of content), if you have chosen to develop a spreadsheet.

- The included spreadsheet project is a competency development task intended to help you synthesize content material by designing a quality improvement program of your choice the way you would have things run in the best of all worlds. The design is communicated in a spreadsheet format. The spreadsheet project is an artifact which you can circulate to colleagues or use as the basis for a talk or presentation event. The philosophy behind this project is that more learning occurs – and learning is more fun – if you can actually build/create something from the content (rather than just being tested on the content) and is useful beyond the reading of this book. There is nothing like being asked to create and present content on a topic to help you learn and think critically about that topic. An example of a spreadsheet project is included in this book in *Appendix B: Spreadsheet Example*.

- There are also trivia questions – just for fun – because everyone also loves little known, but interesting, fun facts.

Appendix A Topic 3. What are the competency objectives for readers?

The overall competency goal of this book is that it **enables you to think more critically and more independently about quality improvement in healthcare organizations in new and interesting ways.**

Specifically, upon successful completion of this book (e.g., the readings, the suggested competency development tasks), you should be able to:

1. Define quality and quality improvement in healthcare organizations

2. Define quality and quality improvement measures in healthcare organizations

3. Define data collection and analysis methodologies for quality and quality improvement measures in healthcare organizations

4. Synthesize course content to create a quality improvement program in a healthcare organization

5. Generate an effective quality improvement spreadsheet suitable for discussion, presentation and printing

The hope embedded in this book is that having achieved these objectives, you do not just know more now that you have read this book, but that you now think more critically and more independently about **healthcare organization quality and quality improvement in new and interesting ways.**

As a result of achieving the competency objectives you should have a better understanding of healthcare organizations and their quality and quality improvement systems. Readers working within a healthcare organization should be better able to contribute to the efficient and effective operations of their organization as a whole as well as the organization's quality and quality improvement system. They will be able to undertake and improve healthcare administration and management responsibilities within their organization.

Appendix A Topic 4. What tasks facilitate achievement of competency objectives?

Competency development tasks include discussion questions, quizzes, and a spreadsheet project. The competency development tasks in this book facilitate content mastery to help you organize your thinking.

Competency development tasks include discussion questions, quizzes, and a spreadsheet project. The competency development tasks in this book facilitate content mastery to help you organize your thinking.

Appendix A Task: Discussion Question

Each discussion question is a competency development task intended to help you consider important and interesting questions related to the readings content. The question is suitable for either discussion with others or your own personal thought and reflection. The purpose of the question is to facilitate critical, independent – as well as possibly new and interesting – ways to think about health care delivery systems.   Each lesson includes at least one discussion question. The discussion questions in this book address the following topics:

- Personal Learning Goal for this Learning Path (Lesson One)

- Relative Quality Importance of the Six Dimensions of Health Care Quality (Lesson One)

- Characteristics of a Great Healthcare Organization Quality Measure (Lesson Two)

- Quality Data Collection Challenges in Healthcare Organizations (Lesson Three)

- Spreadsheet Generation (Lesson Four)

- Achievement of Personal Learning Goal (Lesson Four)

Appendix A Task: Quiz

There are two types of quizzes in this book: content and self-evaluation. Each type of quiz is a competency development task. The first type contains multiple choice or fill-in-the-blank questions based in the designated readings. The purpose of each content quiz is to help you develop competency in the stated study objectives. There is nothing like being asked a question about a topic to help you learn and think critically about that topic. The answer key for each content quiz is at the end of the content quiz. The three content quizzes are:

- Lesson One Quiz
- Lesson Two Quiz
- Lesson Three Quiz

The second type of quiz is a self-evaluation of the spreadsheet project content and format to ensure that you think critically about the spreadsheet (e.g., if the reflects a synthesis of content), if you have chosen to develop a spreadsheet. The two self-evaluation quizzes are:

- Synthesize Content Self-Evaluation (Lesson Four)
- Generate an Effective Spreadsheet Self-Evaluation (Lesson Four)

Appendix A Task: Spreadsheet Project

The included spreadsheet project is a competency development task intended to help you synthesize content material by designing a healthcare organization quality improvement program system of your choice the way you would have things run in the best of all worlds. The design is communicated in a spreadsheet format. The content for the spreadsheet t is your design for a quality improvement system. As such, there are no right or wrong content items. There are only sensible and reasonable items within the content criteria specified in the book. There is also no one right way to organize the spreadsheet format. There are only sensible and reasonable format aspects within the criteria specified in the course of study. Once you have produced the spreadsheet, you should evaluate your spreadsheet using the two self-evaluation quizzes.

The spreadsheet is an artifact which you can circulate to colleagues or use as the basis for a talk or presentation event.   The philosophy behind this project is that more learning occurs – and learning is more fun – if you can actually build/create something from the content (rather than just being tested on the content) and is useful beyond the reading of this book.   There is nothing like being asked to create and present content on a topic to help you learn and think critically about that topic. An example of a spreadsheet project is included in this book in *Appendix B: Spreadsheet Example*.

Appendix A Topic 5. What is the educational philosophy of this book?

The educational philosophy of this book, unlike most other texts, is based in an agenda or purpose aimed at aiding the reader. The book assumes that all readers have their own specific personal goals regarding health care delivery systems in healthcare organizations (e.g., improve health care delivery system skills, improve healthcare administration skills, learn more about healthcare organizations in general). It also assumes that readers have different specific goals.

The primary educational philosophy of the book is, therefore, that readers should be provided with enough content and resources to pursue a personally chosen learning path. Readers should be able to choose a personally customized learning path within the book content which leads to the achievement of personal goals. The provided content should encourage reader independence and critical thinking. Content should extend past the reading of this text and help readers in their chosen work or study. The content of the book should connect readers to the larger world and resources available on the internet.

As such the book provides links to external sites to connect readers to the larger "*real world*" of healthcare organizations to help readers better build their own personal, customized learning path. These links (more than 575) are directly accessible in the content in the e-book version. For the print version – and for reference in the e-book version – the full URL for each link in the book can be found at the corresponding in-text link number *(bib#)* in the section at the end of the book entitled *Bibliography: Associated URL/Link List*. The links also serve as resources which can be used after the book is completed. The list includes data, management, and research links needed for healthcare administration, management, and operations.

Another major philosophical approach of the book is use of the Socratic Method and learning by doing. The Socratic Method promotes understanding of a topic by posing questions on that topic. An answer to the question requires a learner/reader to think critically and synthesize information. Again, reading content is presented as a series of topic questions and answers – the Socratic

Method – because it is a better and much more interesting way for a reader to master content. The project requires readers to synthesize course material to design a healthcare organization and governance structure the way the reader would have things run in the best of all worlds. The philosophy behind this project is that more learning occurs – and learning is more fun – if a reader can actually build/create something from the course of study content (rather than just being tested on the content) and show this built/created artifact to others (learning by doing).

Appendix B: Spreadsheet Example

An example of a spreadsheet containing the seventeen (17) items/criteria suggested earlier is shown below. These seventeen items/criteria include eleven (11) content items/criteria and six (6) design/template items/criteria.

The next four pages show the spreadsheet in a printed 4-page PDF form.

The following four pages show the spreadsheet as it was constructed in Excel.

Overview of the Quality Improvement (QI) Program at Charles Harbor General Hospital (CHGH)
by I.M. Incharge, CEO

Description: CHGH is a private, non-profit, general hospital in Massachusetts. It has an emergency room and a full range of clinical specialties (e.g., internal medicine, general surgery, oncology, cardiology, infectious disease, pediatrics).

QI Framework: Lean Six Sigma because of the focus on first using Lean to eliminate waste in organizational processes and then using Six Sigma to reduce errors by either improving or replacing the processes. It makes little sense to focus on process error before the process is streamlined.

QI Domain Focus: Person-Centeredness. CHGH considers patient/customer satisfaction to be essential to quality at CHGH. A key to patient/customer satisfaction is ensuring that all organizational processes are person-centered.

QI Person-Centeredness Components: CHGH's person-centeredness quality improvement program is aimed at continuously improving the quality of person-centeredness in all aspects of CHGH functioning. To that purpose the quality improvement program is coordinated by the Office of Quality Improvement which actively:

- Views CHGH as a system within which is a system of processes related to ensuring person-centeredness quality. The person-centeredness quality system cuts across all departments and units at CHGH.

- Understands and respects the CHGH patient/customer expectations/requirements of person-centeredness quality when interacting with CHGH.

- Ensures that all CHGH personnel work as a team to improve person-centeredness quality.

Overview of the Quality Improvement (QI) Program at Charles Harbor General Hospital (CHGH)

- Collects and analyzes both qualitative and quantitative data to track person-centeredness quality across all of CHGH.

QI Association Membership: American Society for Quality (ASQ) because of the large array of quality resources available to members.

QI Measure Focus: Outcome measures. For person-centeredness quality, the outcome, the perception of person-centeredness by patients/customers is the key measure. It matters little how hard CHGH tries - what the structure and process are - if the outcome from the perspective of the patient/customer is not of high quality.

QI Primary Measure: Adult Hospital Survey (HCAHPS) which "asks people 18 and older about their experiences with medical, surgical, or obstetric care provided in an inpatient setting". This was chosen because it is used by more than 4000 hospitals in the United States which means it is reliable and valid and allows for benchmarking. Personnel from the Office of Quality Improvement also monitor reviews on such sites as Yelp and respond as necessary. Personnel also visit patient/customer waiting areas and informally ask some patients/customers on a daily basis to provide informal feedback.

QI Data Type: Ordinal. The HCAHPS Survey contains 21 patient perspectives on care and patient rating items that encompass nine key topics: communication with doctors, communication with nurses, responsiveness of hospital staff, pain management, communication about medicines, discharge information, cleanliness of the hospital environment, quietness of the hospital environment, and transition of care (https://www.hcahpsonline.org/). The survey can be found at https://www.hcahpsonline.org/en/survey-instruments/ and the answers to the questions are generally coded 1, 2, 3, and 4, where the lower the number the lower the quality. Answers coded 1 and 2 could be considered to be indicative of low quality.

2

Overview of the Quality Improvement (QI) Program at Charles Harbor General Hospital (CHGH)

QI Data Collection: The HCAPHS survey is mailed to all patients discharged from CHGH within three days of discharge. The survey is 32 questions in length. There are four approved modes of administration for the CAHPS Hospital Survey: 1) Mail Only; 2) Telephone Only; 3) Mixed (mail followed by telephone); and 4) Active Interactive Voice Response (IVR).

QI Data Analysis: The topics of the HCAPHS survey which CHGH considers related to person-centeredness are: communication with doctors, communication with nurses, responsiveness of hospital staff, communication about medicines, and discharge information. A Pareto Chart is used to display and analyze this information.

For the purposes of this assignment, the relevant data for each chosen topic are the number of patient/customers whose response was either a 1 or a 2. Of 100 surveyed patients/customers, the number who gave a 1 or a 2 to: communication with doctors (Com Doc) = 45, communication with nurses (Com Nur) = 52, responsiveness of hospital staff (Res HSt) = 31, communication about medicines (Com Med)= 21, and discharge information (Dis Inf) = 65.

Topic	Number	Percent
Dis Inf	65	30
Com Nur	52	54
Com Doc	45	75
Res HSt	31	90
Com Med	21	100

Conclusion: More than half of the complaints can be elminated or reduced by focusing quality improvement efforts on improving Dis Inf (Discharge Information) and Com Nur (Communication with Nurses).

Overview of the Quality Improvement (QI) Program at Charles Harbor General Hospital (CHGH)

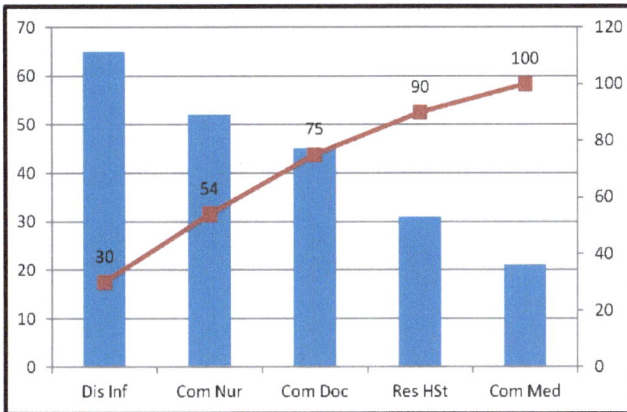

4

Excel Rows 1 to 14

	A	B	C	D	E	F	G	H
1	**Overview of the Quality Improvement (QI) Program at Charles Harbor General Hospital (CHGH)**							
2	by I.M. Incharge, CEO							
3								
4	**Description:** CHGH is a private, non-profit, general hospital in Massachusetts. It has an emergency room and a full range of clinical specialties (e.g., internal medicine, general surgery, oncology, cardiology, infectious disease, pediatrics).							
5								
6	**QI Framework:** Lean Six Sigma because of the focus on first using Lean to eliminate waste in organizational processes and then using Six Sigma to reduce errors by either improving or replacing the processes. It makes little sense to focus on process error before the process is streamlined.							
7								
8	**QI Domain Focus:** Person-Centeredness. CHGH considers patient/customer satisfaction to be essential to quality at CHGH. A key to patient/customer satisfaction is ensuring that all organizational processes are person-centered.							
9								
10	**QI Person-Centeredness Components:** CHGH's person-centeredness quality improvement program is aimed at continuously improving the quality of person-centeredness in all aspects of CHGH functioning. To that purpose the quality improvement program is coordinated by the Office of Quality Improvement which actively:							
11		• Views CHGH as a system within which is a system of processes related to ensuring person-centeredness quality. The person-centeredness quality system cuts across all departments and units at CHGH.							
12		• Understands and respects the CHGH patient/customer expectations/requirements of person-centeredness quality when interacting with CHGH.							
13		• Ensures that all CHGH personnel work as a team to improve person-centeredness quality.							
14		• Collects and analyzes both qualitative and quantitative data to track person-centeredness quality across all of CHGH.							

	A	B	C	D	E	F	G	H
15								
16	**QI Assocation Membership:** American Society for Quality (ASQ) because of the large array of quality resources available to members.							
17								
18	**QI Measure Focus:** Outcome measures. For person-centeredness quality, the outcome, the perception of person-centeredness by patients/customers is the key measure. It matters little how hard CHGH tries - what the structure and process are - if the outcome from the perspective of the patient/customer is not of high quality.							
19								
20	**QI Primary Measure:** Adult Hospital Survey (HCAHPS) which "asks people 18 and older about their experiences with medical, surgical, or obstetric care provided in an inpatient setting". This was chosen because it is used by more than 4000 hospitals in the United States which means it is reliable and valid and allows for benchmarking. Personnel from the Office of Quality Improvement also monitor reviews on such sites as Yelp and respond as necessary. Personnel also visit patient/customer waiting areas and informally ask some patients/customers on a daily basis to provide informal feedback.							
21								
22	**QI Data Type:** Ordinal. The HCAHPS Survey contains 21 patient perspectives on care and patient rating items that encompass nine key topics: communication with doctors, communication with nurses, responsiveness of hospital staff, pain management, communication about medicines, discharge information, cleanliness of the hospital environment, quietness of the hospital environment, and transition of care (https://www.hcahpsonline.org/). The survey can be found at https://www.hcahpsonline.org/en/survey-instruments/ and the answers to the questions are generally coded 1, 2, 3, and 4, where the lower the number the lower the quality. Answers coded 1 and 2 could be considered to be indicative of low quality.							
23								
24	**QI Data Collection:** The HCAPHS survey is mailed to all patients discharged from CHGH within three days of discharge. The survey is 32 questions in length. There are four approved modes of administration for the CAHPS Hospital Survey: 1) Mail Only; 2) Telephone Only; 3) Mixed (mail followed by telephone); and 4) Active Interactive Voice Response (IVR).							
25								

	A	B	C	D	E	F	G	H
26	**QI Data Analysis**: The topics of the HCAPHS survey which CHGH considers related to person-centeredness are: communication with doctors, communication with nurses, responsiveness of hospital staff, communication about medicines, and discharge information. A Pareto Chart is used to display and analyze this information.							
27								
28	**For the purposes of this assignment**, the relevant data for each chosen topic are the number of patient/customers whose response was either a 1 or a 2. Of 100 surveyed patients/customers, the number who gave a 1 or a 2 to: communication with doctors (Com Doc) = 45, communication with nurses (Com Nur) = 52, responsiveness of hospital staff (Res HSt) = 31, communication about medicines (Com Med)= 21, and discharge information (Dis Inf) = 65.							
29								
30	Topic	Number	Percent					
31	Dis Inf	65	30					
32	Com Nur	52	54					
33	Com Doc	45	75					
34	Res HSt	31	90					
35	Com Med	21	100					
36								
37	**Conclusion:** More than half of the complaints can be elminated or reduced by focusing quality improvement efforts on improving Dis Inf (Discharge Information) and Com Nur (Communication with Nurses).							
38								
39								
40								
41								
42								
43								
44								
45								
46								
47								
48								
49								
50								

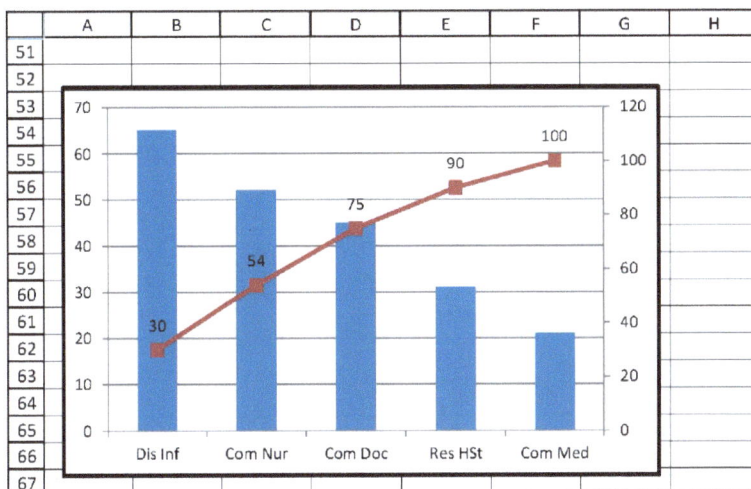

Bibliography: Associated URL/Link List

1. Book Text: *history of the healthcare quality movement* Link Associated with Text: https://www.ncbi.nlm.nih.gov/pmc/articles/PMC3702754/
2. Book Text: *Ignaz Semmelweis* Link Associated with Text: https://en.wikipedia.org/wiki/Ignaz_Semmelweis
3. Book Text: *John Snow* Link Associated with Text: http://www.ph.ucla.edu/epi/snow.html
4. Book Text: *removed the handle of the Broad Street Pump* Link Associated with Text: http://www.ph.ucla.edu/epi/snow/removal.html
5. Book Text: *Ernest Codman, MD* Link Associated with Text: https://en.wikipedia.org/wiki/Ernest_Amory_Codman
6. Book Text: *American College of Surgeons (ACS)* Link Associated with Text: https://www.facs.org/
7. Book Text: *him fired from MGH in 1914* Link Associated with Text: http://history.massgeneral.org/catalog/Detail.aspx?itemId=1352&searchFor=Books%20and%20Documents
8. Book Text: *Florence Nightingale* Link Associated with Text: https://en.wikipedia.org/wiki/Florence_Nightingale
9. Book Text: *Crimean War* Link Associated with Text: https://en.wikipedia.org/wiki/Crimean_War
10. Book Text: *one of her coxcombs* Link Associated with Text: https://commons.wikimedia.org/wiki/File:Nightingale-mortality.jpg
11. Book Text: *member of the International Statistical Institute (ISI)* Link Associated with Text: https://www.isi-web.org/index.php/about-isi/what-is-isi/history
12. Book Text: *Fellow of the Royal Statistical Society* Link Associated with Text: https://rss.org.uk/news-publication/news-publications/2020/general-news/nightingale-2020-the-bicentenary-our-first-female/
13. Book Text: *American Statistical Association* Link Associated with Text: http://thisisstatistics.org/florence-nightingale-the-lady-with-the-data/
14. Book Text: *Chicago Public Library* Link Associated with Text: https://www.chipublib.org/
15. Book Text: *Winter Garden, Harold Washington Library* Link Associated with Text: https://www.chipublib.org/news/your-new-favorite-study-space-winter-garden-at-harold-washington-library-center/
16. Book Text: *Image from Wikipedia, File:9th Level Harold Washington Library.jpg* Link Associated with Text: https://en.wikipedia.org/wiki/File:9th_Level_Harold_Washington_Library.jpg
17. Book Text: *Seattle Public Library* Link Associated with Text: https://www.spl.org/
18. Book Text: *Central Library* Link Associated with Text: https://www.spl.org/hours-and-locations/central-library
19. Book Text: *New York Public Library* Link Associated with Text: https://www.nypl.org/

20. Book Text: *Rose Main Reading Room, Stephen A. Schwarzman Building*
    Link Associated with Text:
    https://www.nypl.org/about/divisions/general-research-division/rose-main-reading-room
21. Book Text: *Image from Wikipedia, File:NYC Public Library Research Room Jan 2006.jpg (Photo by DAVID ILIFF. License: CC-BY-SA 3.0)*
    Link Associated with Text:
    https://en.wikipedia.org/wiki/File:NYC_Public_Library_Research_Room_Jan_2006.jpg
22. Book Text: *Video: What Do You Know About the Golden Gate Bridge?*
    Link Associated with Text:
    https://www.youtube.com/watch?v=6HygbD44_j4
23. Book Text: *Historic Landmarks* Link Associated with Text:
    https://www.asce.org/landmarks/#
24. Book Text: *defines quality* Link Associated with Text:
    https://www.merriam-webster.com/dictionary/quality
25. Book Text: *defines quality with respect to a manufacturing organization*
    Link Associated with Text:
    http://www.businessdictionary.com/definition/quality.html
26. Book Text: *health care quality* Link Associated with Text:
    http://www.nationalacademies.org/hmd/Global/News%20Announcements/Crossing-the-Quality-Chasm-The-IOM-Health-Care-Quality-Initiative.aspx
27. Book Text: *Johns Hopkins study* Link Associated with Text:
    https://www.hopkinsmedicine.org/news/media/releases/study_suggests_medical_errors_now_third_leading_cause_of_death_in_the_us
28. Book Text: *Medical error* Link Associated with Text:
    https://www.bmj.com/content/353/bmj.i2139.full
29. Book Text: *MedWatch* Link Associated with Text:
    https://www.fda.gov/safety/medwatch/default.htm
30. Book Text: *medication error* Link Associated with Text:
    https://www.nccmerp.org/about-medication-errors
31. Book Text: *Video: MedWatch Tips & Tools* Link Associated with Text:
    https://www.youtube.com/watch?v=7b-fcRQ2Q7k
32. Book Text: *medical malpractice claim* Link Associated with Text:
    https://en.wikipedia.org/wiki/Medical_malpractice_in_the_United_States
33. Book Text: *17,000 medical malpractice* Link Associated with Text:
    https://www.forbes.com/sites/amino/2016/04/19/does-your-doctor-have-malpractice-claims-how-to-find-out/#31dfef555a64
34. Book Text: *estimated that* Link Associated with Text:
    https://www.nejm.org/doi/full/10.1056/NEJMsa1012370
35. Book Text: *Defensive medicine* Link Associated with Text:
    https://www.verywellhealth.com/defensive-medicine-2615160
36. Book Text: *practice of defensive medicine* Link Associated with Text:
    https://www.policymed.com/2010/09/defensive-medicine-adds-45-billion-to-the-cost-of-healthcare.html

37. Book Text: *medical liability tort reform* Link Associated with Text:
https://www.verywellhealth.com/what-is-tort-reform-1736101

38. Book Text: *More than half* Link Associated with Text:
https://www.merritthawkins.com/news-and-insights/blog/healthcare-news-trends/which-states-have-tort-reform-where-to-practice/

39. Book Text: *defines QI* Link Associated with Text:
https://www.hrsa.gov/sites/default/files/quality/toolbox/508pdfs/qualityimprovement.pdf

40. Book Text: *Quality Assurance (QA)* Link Associated with Text:
https://en.wikipedia.org/wiki/Quality_assurance

41. Book Text: *QI program* Link Associated with Text:
https://www.hrsa.gov/sites/default/files/quality/toolbox/508pdfs/qualityimprovement.pdf

42. Book Text: *Chronic Care Model (CCM)* Link Associated with Text:
http://www.improvingchroniccare.org/index.php?p=The_Chronic_Care_Model&s=2

43. Book Text: *Health System* Link Associated with Text:
http://www.improvingchroniccare.org/index.php?p=Health_System&s=20

44. Book Text: *Delivery System Design* Link Associated with Text:
http://www.improvingchroniccare.org/index.php?p=Delivery_System_Design&s=21

45. Book Text: *Decision Support* Link Associated with Text:
http://www.improvingchroniccare.org/index.php?p=Decision_Support&s=24

46. Book Text: *Clinical Information Systems* Link Associated with Text:
http://www.improvingchroniccare.org/index.php?p=Clinical_Information_Systems&s=25

47. Book Text: *Self-Management Support* Link Associated with Text:
http://www.improvingchroniccare.org/index.php?p=Self-Management_Support&s=22

48. Book Text: *The Community* Link Associated with Text:
http://www.improvingchroniccare.org/index.php?p=The_Community&s=19

49. Book Text: *Lean Model* Link Associated with Text:
https://www.virginiamasoninstitute.org/training-services/foundations-of-lean-in-health-care/

50. Book Text: *Lean Health Care* Link Associated with Text:
https://www.virginiamasoninstitute.org/2017/08/lean-health-care/

51. Book Text: *Toyota Production System* Link Associated with Text:
https://en.wikipedia.org/wiki/Toyota_Production_System

52. Book Text: *was inspired by* Link Associated with Text:
https://www.lean.org/WhatsLean/History.cfm

53. Book Text: *Henry Ford* Link Associated with Text:
https://en.wikipedia.org/wiki/Henry_Ford

54. Book Text: *moving assembly line* Link Associated with Text:
https://www.asme.org/engineering-topics/articles/automotive/henry-ford

55. Book Text: *Video: The 8 Wastes in Health Care* Link Associated with Text: https://www.youtube.com/watch?v=7mA1L_a_FX4
56. Book Text: *What is Lean Healthcare?* Link Associated with Text: https://catalyst.nejm.org/what-is-lean-healthcare/
57. Book Text: *Lean Principles in Healthcare: 2 Important Tools Organizations Must Have* Link Associated with Text: https://www.healthcatalyst.com/lean-principles-in-healthcare-2-key-tools
58. Book Text: *Lean Enterprise Institute* Link Associated with Text: https://www.lean.org/
59. Book Text: *Going Lean in Healthcare* Link Associated with Text: https://www.entnet.org/sites/default/files/GoingLeaninHealthCareWhitePaper-3.pdf
60. Book Text: *Lean* Link Associated with Text: https://www.niddk.nih.gov/health-information/communication-programs/ndep/health-professionals/practice-transformation-physicians-health-care-teams/techniques-improving-quality-care/quality-improvement-methodologies/lean
61. Book Text: *Lean Management—The Journey from Toyota to Healthcare* Link Associated with Text: https://www.ncbi.nlm.nih.gov/pmc/articles/PMC3678835/
62. Book Text: *Six Sigma* Link Associated with Text: https://en.wikipedia.org/wiki/Six_Sigma
63. Book Text: *Six Sigma error rate* Link Associated with Text: https://www.niddk.nih.gov/health-information/communication-programs/ndep/health-professionals/practice-transformation-physicians-health-care-teams/techniques-improving-quality-care/quality-improvement-methodologies/six-sigma
64. Book Text: *DMAIC* Link Associated with Text: http://asq.org/learn-about-quality/six-sigma/overview/dmaic.html
65. Book Text: *DMADV* Link Associated with Text: https://www.sixsigmadaily.com/what-is-dmadv/
66. Book Text: *Six Sigma was developed at Motorola* Link Associated with Text: https://en.wikipedia.org/wiki/Six_Sigma
67. Book Text: *What is Six Sigma?* Link Associated with Text: http://asq.org/learn-about-quality/six-sigma/overview/overview.html
68. Book Text: *About Six Sigma* Link Associated with Text: https://www.6sigma.us/six-sigma.php
69. Book Text: *Lean Six Sigma Institute (LSSI)* Link Associated with Text: http://www.leansixsigmainstitute.org/
70. Book Text: *Lean Six Sigma in Healthcare* Link Associated with Text: http://asq.org/healthcaresixsigma/lean-six-sigma.html
71. Book Text: *The Applicability of Lean and Six Sigma Techniques to Clinical and Translational Research* Link Associated with Text: https://www.ncbi.nlm.nih.gov/pmc/articles/PMC2835466/

72. Book Text: *Lean and Six Sigma in Acute Care: A Systematic Review of Reviews* Link Associated with Text: https://www.ncbi.nlm.nih.gov/pubmed/26959898
73. Book Text: *Which Is Better for Engaging Health Care Staff: Lean or Six Sigma* Link Associated with Text: https://www.virginiamasoninstitute.org/2016/02/better-engaging-health-care-staff-lean-six-sigma/
74. Book Text: *Model for Improvement* Link Associated with Text: http://www.ihi.org/resources/Pages/HowtoImprove/default.aspx
75. Book Text: *Institute for Healthcare Improvement* Link Associated with Text: http://www.ihi.org/resources/Pages/HowtoImprove/default.aspx
76. Book Text: *API* Link Associated with Text: http://www.apiweb.org/
77. Book Text: *Setting Aims* Link Associated with Text: http://www.ihi.org/resources/Pages/HowtoImprove/ScienceofImprovementSettingAims.aspx
78. Book Text: *Establishing Measures* Link Associated with Text: http://www.ihi.org/resources/Pages/HowtoImprove/ScienceofImprovementEstablishingMeasures.aspx
79. Book Text: *Selecting Changes* Link Associated with Text: http://www.ihi.org/resources/Pages/HowtoImprove/ScienceofImprovementSelectingChanges.aspx
80. Book Text: *Testing the changes* Link Associated with Text: http://www.ihi.org/resources/Pages/HowtoImprove/ScienceofImprovementTestingChanges.aspx
81. Book Text: *Institute for Healthcare Improvement (IHI) Model for Improvement* Link Associated with Text: https://www.niddk.nih.gov/health-information/communication-programs/ndep/health-professionals/practice-transformation-physicians-health-care-teams/techniques-improving-quality-care/quality-improvement-methodologies/ihi-model-improvement
82. Book Text: *Examples of PDSA Cycles for Quality Improvement Activities to Address Elements of the Chronic Care Model* Link Associated with Text:
83. Book Text: *Example for Improving Diabetes Management using PDSA Cycle Process* Link Associated with Text: https://www.niddk.nih.gov/-/media/Files/Health-Information/Communication-Programs/NDEP/health-care-professionals/Table_2-Examples_for_Improving_Diabetes_Mangament-updated.pdf?la=en
84. Book Text: *Crossing the Global Quality Chasm: Improving Health Care Worldwide* Link Associated with Text: https://www.nap.edu/read/25152/chapter/1
85. Book Text: *Health and Medicine Division* Link Associated with Text: https://www.nap.edu/author/HMD
86. Book Text: *Board on Global Health* Link Associated with Text: https://www.nap.edu/author/BGH

87. Book Text: *Board on Health Care Services* Link Associated with Text: https://www.nap.edu/author/HCS
88. Book Text: *Committee on Improving the Quality of Health Care Globally* Link Associated with Text: https://www.nap.edu/initiative/committee-on-improving-the-quality-of-health-care-globally
89. Book Text: *Crossing the Quality Chasm: A New Health System for the 21st Century* Link Associated with Text: https://www.nap.edu/catalog/10027/crossing-the-quality-chasm-a-new-health-system-for-the
90. Book Text: *National Academies* Link Associated with Text: http://www.nationalacademies.org/
91. Book Text: *purpose is to* Link Associated with Text: http://www.nasonline.org/about-nas/mission/
92. Book Text: *signed into law* Link Associated with Text: http://www.nasonline.org/about-nas/history/
93. Book Text: *NAE* Link Associated with Text: https://www.nae.edu/
94. Book Text: *was founded in 1970* Link Associated with Text: https://nam.edu/
95. Book Text: *NRC* Link Associated with Text: http://www.nasonline.org/about-nas/history/archives/milestones-in-NAS-history/organization-of-the-nrc.html
96. Book Text: *Studies and reports* Link Associated with Text: http://www.nationalacademies.org/about/advice/index.html
97. Book Text: *seven program* Link Associated with Text: http://www.nationalacademies.org/nasem/
98. Book Text: *HMD* Link Associated with Text: http://www.nationalacademies.org/hmd/
99. Book Text: *Quality and Patient Safety* Link Associated with Text: http://www.nationalacademies.org/hmd/Global/Topics/quality-patient-safety.aspx
100. Book Text: *TeamSTEPPS* Link Associated with Text: https://www.ahrq.gov/teamstepps/index.html
101. Book Text: *Video: Successful Outcome Using TeamSTEPPS Techniques* Link Associated with Text: https://www.youtube.com/watch?v=yWd56QVL1VQ
102. Book Text: *Clean hands* Link Associated with Text: https://www.cdc.gov/features/handhygiene/index.html
103. Book Text: *HAI* Link Associated with Text: https://www.cdc.gov/hai/
104. Book Text: *about one in 31 hospital patients* Link Associated with Text: https://www.cdc.gov/hai/data/index.html
105. Book Text: *puerperal fever* Link Associated with Text: https://en.wikipedia.org/wiki/Puerperal_fever
106. Book Text: *of an infection* Link Associated with Text: https://www.npr.org/sections/health-shots/2015/01/12/375663920/the-doctor-who-championed-hand-washing-and-saved-women-s-lives

107. Book Text: *Semmelweis Reflex* Link Associated with Text: https://en.wikipedia.org/wiki/Semmelweis_reflex
108. Book Text: *Clinical Decision Support* Link Associated with Text: https://www.ahrq.gov/professionals/prevention-chronic-care/decision/clinical/index.html
109. Book Text: *CDS* Link Associated with Text: https://www.healthit.gov/topic/safety/clinical-decision-support
110. Book Text: *Healthy People 2020* Link Associated with Text: https://www.healthypeople.gov/
111. Book Text: *Access to Health Services* Link Associated with Text: https://www.healthypeople.gov/2020/topics-objectives/topic/Access-to-Health-Services
112. Book Text: *National health expenditures* Link Associated with Text: https://www.cms.gov/research-statistics-data-and-systems/statistics-trends-and-reports/nationalhealthexpenddata/nhe-fact-sheet.html
113. Book Text: *an interest area* Link Associated with Text: https://www.healthypeople.gov/2020/about/foundation-health-measures/Disparities
114. Book Text: *NIST* Link Associated with Text: https://www.nist.gov/
115. Book Text: *ASQ* Link Associated with Text: https://asq.org/about-asq
116. Book Text: *in 1901* Link Associated with Text: https://www.nist.gov/timeline#event-a-href-node-774241nist-founded-a
117. Book Text: *Baldrige Performance Excellence Program* Link Associated with Text: https://www.nist.gov/baldrige
118. Book Text: *Health and Bioscience Division* Link Associated with Text: https://www.nist.gov/topics/health-bioscience
119. Book Text: *Health and Biological Systems Measurement* Link Associated with Text: https://www.nist.gov/industry-impacts/health-and-biological-systems-measurement
120. Book Text: *vaccine storage* Link Associated with Text: https://www.nist.gov/industry-impacts/reliable-vaccine-storage
121. Book Text: *Baldrige Excellence Framework* Link Associated with Text: https://www.nist.gov/baldrige/publications/baldrige-excellence-framework
122. Book Text: *Health Care* Link Associated with Text: https://www.nist.gov/baldrige/publications/baldrige-excellence-framework/health-care
123. Book Text: *Criteria* Link Associated with Text: https://www.nist.gov/baldrige/about-baldrige-excellence-framework-health-care
124. Book Text: *improvement tools* Link Associated with Text: https://www.nist.gov/baldrige/self-assessing/improvement-tools
125. Book Text: *easyInsight: Take a First Step toward a Baldrige Self-Assessment For Health Care Organizations* Link Associated with Text: https://wsw680p01.nist.gov/easyInsight/index.cfm?ct=hc

126. Book Text: *Malcolm Baldrige National Quality Award* Link Associated with Text: https://www.nist.gov/baldrige/baldrige-award
127. Book Text: *One award sector is Health Care* Link Associated with Text: https://www.nist.gov/baldrige/award-recipients?field_baldrige_award_year_value_selective=All&field_baldrige_sector_tid=1939011&title=&field_baldrige_state_tid=All
128. Book Text: *Memorial Hospital and Health Care Center* Link Associated with Text: https://www.nist.gov/baldrige/memorial-hospital-and-health-care-center
129. Book Text: *Adventist Health Castle* Link Associated with Text: https://www.nist.gov/baldrige/adventist-health-castle
130. Book Text: *Southcentral Foundation* Link Associated with Text: https://www.nist.gov/baldrige/southcentral-foundation-2017
131. Book Text: *administers* Link Associated with Text: http://asq.org/learn-about-quality/malcolm-baldrige-award/overview/overview.html
132. Book Text: *Publishing journals* Link Associated with Text: http://asq.org/pub/
133. Book Text: *Quality Progress* Link Associated with Text: http://asq.org/qualityprogress/
134. Book Text: *Quality Resources* Link Associated with Text: https://asq.org/quality-resources
135. Book Text: *Professional certifications* Link Associated with Text: https://asq.org/cert/catalog
136. Book Text: *CQA* Link Associated with Text: https://asq.org/cert/quality-auditor
137. Book Text: *CBA* Link Associated with Text: https://asq.org/cert/biomedical-auditor
138. Book Text: *CPGP* Link Associated with Text: https://asq.org/cert/pharmaceutical-gmp
139. Book Text: *Video: ASQ TV Episode 2: Culture of Quality* Link Associated with Text: https://www.youtube.com/watch?v=VsSk_S226HM
140. Book Text: *AHRQ* Link Associated with Text: https://www.ahrq.gov/cpi/about/profile/index.html
141. Book Text: *IHI* Link Associated with Text: http://www.ihi.org/about/pages/ihivisionandvalues.aspx
142. Book Text: *NCQA* Link Associated with Text: https://www.ncqa.org/
143. Book Text: *NAHQ* Link Associated with Text: https://nahq.org/
144. Book Text: *PHF* Link Associated with Text: http://www.phf.org/Pages/default.aspx
145. Book Text: *NACCHO* Link Associated with Text: https://www.naccho.org/
146. Book Text: *PQA* Link Associated with Text: https://www.pqaalliance.org/
147. Book Text: *CMS* Link Associated with Text: https://www.cms.gov/
148. Book Text: *FDA* Link Associated with Text: https://www.fda.gov/

149. Book Text: *Data* Link Associated with Text: https://www.ahrq.gov/data/index.html
150. Book Text: *Tools* Link Associated with Text: https://www.ahrq.gov/tools/index.html
151. Book Text: *CPPS* Link Associated with Text: http://www.ihi.org/education/cpps-certified-professional-in-patient-safety/Pages/default.aspx
152. Book Text: *Physician and Hospital Quality Certification* Link Associated with Text: https://www.ncqa.org/programs/health-plans/physician-and-hospital-quality-phq/faqs/all/
153. Book Text: *Quality Talks* Link Associated with Text: http://www.qualitytalks.org/quality-talks-overview/
154. Book Text: *HEDIS* Link Associated with Text: https://www.ncqa.org/hedis/
155. Book Text: *Healthcare Quality Week* Link Associated with Text: https://nahq.org/about/healthcare-quality-week
156. Book Text: *HQF* Link Associated with Text: https://nahq.org/about/healthcare-quality-foundation
157. Book Text: *CPHQ* Link Associated with Text: https://nahq.org/certification/certified-professional-healthcare-quality
158. Book Text: *Quality Improvement in Public Health* Link Associated with Text: http://www.phf.org/focusareas/qualityimprovement/Pages/Quality_Improvement.aspx
159. Book Text: *Quality Improvement Resources* Link Associated with Text: http://www.phf.org/focusareas/qualityimprovement/Pages/Quality_Improvement_Resources.aspx
160. Book Text: *QI Quick Guide* Link Associated with Text: http://www.phf.org/focusareas/qualityimprovement/QIQuickGuide/Pages/Welcome_to_the_Guide_to_Quality_Improvement.aspx
161. Book Text: *Quality Improvement Tools* Link Associated with Text: http://www.phf.org/programs/QItools/Pages/Quality_Improvement_Tools_to_Advance_Public_Health_Performance.aspx
162. Book Text: *Quality Improvement* Link Associated with Text: https://www.naccho.org/programs/public-health-infrastructure/performance-improvement/quality-improvement
163. Book Text: *performance measures* Link Associated with Text: https://www.pqaalliance.org/pqa-measures
164. Book Text: *Quality Forum Series* Link Associated with Text: https://www.pqaalliance.org/quality-forum-series-main
165. Book Text: *Quality Awards* Link Associated with Text: https://www.pqaalliance.org/pqa-awards-program
166. Book Text: *Quality Initiatives* Link Associated with Text: https://www.cms.gov/Medicare/Quality-Initiatives-Patient-Assessment-Instruments/QualityInitiativesGenInfo/index.html

167. Book Text: *Meaningful Measures Framework* Link Associated with Text: https://www.cms.gov/Medicare/Quality-Initiatives-Patient-Assessment-Instruments/QualityInitiativesGenInfo/CMS-Quality-Strategy.html

168. Book Text: *maintain quality in the process* Link Associated with Text: https://www.fda.gov/MedicalDevices/DeviceRegulationandGuidance/MedicalDeviceQualityandCompliance/ucm378185.htm

169. Book Text: *Quality System (QS) Regulation/Medical Device Good Manufacturing Practices* Link Associated with Text: https://www.fda.gov/medical-devices/postmarket-requirements-devices/quality-system-qs-regulationmedical-device-good-manufacturing-practices

170. Book Text: *Pharmaceutical Quality Resources* Link Associated with Text: https://www.fda.gov/Drugs/DevelopmentApprovalProcess/Manufacturing/default.htm

171. Book Text: *CDRH Quality Management Program* Link Associated with Text: https://www.fda.gov/AboutFDA/CentersOffices/OfficeofMedicalProductsandTobacco/CDRH/CDRHQualityManagementProgram/default.htm

172. Book Text: *Quality Measures* Link Associated with Text: https://www.cms.gov/Medicare/Quality-Initiatives-Patient-Assessment-Instruments/QualityMeasures/index.html

173. Book Text: *Quality Measures as measures* Link Associated with Text: https://www.ahrq.gov/professionals/quality-patient-safety/talkingquality/create/types.html

174. Book Text: *Donabedian Model* Link Associated with Text: https://en.wikipedia.org/wiki/Donabedian_model

175. Book Text: *Avedis Donabedian* Link Associated with Text: https://en.wikipedia.org/wiki/Avedis_Donabedian

176. Book Text: *Evaluating the quality of medical care* Link Associated with Text: https://www.milbank.org/quarterly/articles/evaluating-quality-medical-care/

177. Book Text: *defines such an outcome measure* Link Associated with Text: https://www.who.int/healthpromotion/about/HPR Glossary 1998.pdf

178. Book Text: *Pierre-Charles-Alexandre Louis* Link Associated with Text: https://en.wikipedia.org/wiki/Pierre_Charles_Alexandre_Louis

179. Book Text: *outcome of blood-letting* Link Associated with Text: https://www.ncbi.nlm.nih.gov/pmc/articles/PMC1383766/#ref5

180. Book Text: *Researches On The Effects Of Bloodletting In Some Inflammatory Diseases* Link Associated with Text: https://archive.org/details/researchesoneffe00louiuoft/page/n5

181. Book Text: *inventor of the numerical method in medicine* Link Associated with Text: http://brought tolife.sciencemuseum.org.uk/broughttolife/people/pierrecharlesalexandrelouis

182. Book Text: *Video: Outcome measures: Attributing a score* Link Associated with Text: https://www.youtube.com/watch?v=1pnC7W93YeY
183. Book Text: *NQF* Link Associated with Text: http://www.qualityforum.org/About_NQF/
184. Book Text: *Measure Evaluation Criteria* Link Associated with Text: http://www.qualityforum.org/measuring_performance/submitting_standards/measure_evaluation_criteria.aspx
185. Book Text: *Measures, Reports & Tools* Link Associated with Text: https://www.qualityforum.org/Measures_Reports_Tools.aspx
186. Book Text: *QPS* Link Associated with Text: http://www.qualityforum.org/QPS/QPSTool.aspx
187. Book Text: *MMS* Link Associated with Text: https://www.cms.gov/Medicare/Quality-Initiatives-Patient-Assessment-Instruments/MMS/Index.html
188. Book Text: *CMS Quality Measures Inventory* Link Associated with Text: https://www.cms.gov/Medicare/Quality-Initiatives-Patient-Assessment-Instruments/QualityMeasures/CMS-Measures-Inventory.html
189. Book Text: *ONC* Link Associated with Text: https://www.healthit.gov/topic/about-onc
190. Book Text: *eCQI* Link Associated with Text: https://ecqi.healthit.gov/content/about-ecqi
191. Book Text: *Eligible Hospital/Critical Access Hospital eCQMs* Link Associated with Text: https://ecqi.healthit.gov/eligible-hospital-critical-access-hospital-ecqms
192. Book Text: *Eligible Professional/Eligible Clinician eCQMs* Link Associated with Text: https://ecqi.healthit.gov/eligible-professional-eligible-clinician-ecqms
193. Book Text: *NQF2372* Link Associated with Text: http://www.qualityforum.org/QPS/MeasureDetails.aspx?standardID=2372&print=0&entityTypeID=1
194. Book Text: *CMIT5779* Link Associated with Text: https://cmit.cms.gov/CMIT_public/ViewMeasure?MeasureId=5779
195. Book Text: *eCQM CMS125v7* Link Associated with Text: https://ecqi.healthit.gov/ecqm/measures/cms125v7
196. Book Text: *Benchmarking* Link Associated with Text: https://www.aafp.org/practice-management/improvement/measures.html
197. Book Text: *is useful* Link Associated with Text: https://www.healthcatalyst.com/healthcare-benchmarking/
198. Book Text: *Calc* Link Associated with Text: https://www.libreoffice.org/discover/calc/
199. Book Text: *LibreOffice* Link Associated with Text: https://www.libreoffice.org/
200. Book Text: *U.S. Department of Education, Family Educational Rights and Privacy Act (FERPA)* Link Associated with Text: https://www2.ed.gov/policy/gen/guid/fpco/ferpa/index.html

201. Book Text: *Wikipedia, Family Educational Rights and Privacy Act* Link Associated with Text: https://en.wikipedia.org/wiki/Family_Educational_Rights_and_Privacy_Act
202. Book Text: *Boston Latin School* Link Associated with Text: https://www.bls.org/apps/pages/index.jsp?uREC_ID=206116&type=d
203. Book Text: *National Gallery of Art* Link Associated with Text: https://www.nga.gov/
204. Book Text: *Video: The Mount Maker* Link Associated with Text: https://www.youtube.com/watch?v=ORIs2HiwHzg
205. Book Text: *receive Medicaid funds* Link Associated with Text: https://www.macpac.gov/subtopic/key-federal-program-accountability-requirements-in-medicaid-managed-care/
206. Book Text: *Quality of Care* Link Associated with Text: https://www.medicaid.gov/medicaid/quality-of-care/index.html
207. Book Text: *Child Core Set* Link Associated with Text: https://www.medicaid.gov/medicaid/quality-of-care/performance-measurement/child-core-set/index.html
208. Book Text: *Medicaid Quality Improvement Initiatives* Link Associated with Text: https://www.medicaid.gov/medicaid/quality-of-care/improvement-initiatives/index.html
209. Book Text: *Adult Core Set* Link Associated with Text: https://www.medicaid.gov/medicaid/quality-of-care/performance-measurement/adult-core-set/index.html
210. Book Text: *CAHPS* Link Associated with Text: https://www.medicaid.gov/medicaid/quality-of-care/performance-measurement/adult-cahps/index.html
211. Book Text: *NQS* Link Associated with Text: https://www.ahrq.gov/workingforquality/about/index.html
212. Book Text: *The Core Quality Measures Collaborative* Link Associated with Text: https://www.cms.gov/Medicare/Quality-Initiatives-Patient-Assessment-Instruments/QualityMeasures/Core-Measures.html
213. Book Text: *Accountable Care Organizations (ACOs), Patient Centered Medical Homes (PCMH), and Primary Care* Link Associated with Text: https://www.cms.gov/Medicare/Quality-Initiatives-Patient-Assessment-Instruments/QualityMeasures/Downloads/ACO-and-PCMH-Primary-Care-Measures.pdf
214. Book Text: *Cardiology* Link Associated with Text: https://www.cms.gov/Medicare/Quality-Initiatives-Patient-Assessment-Instruments/QualityMeasures/Downloads/Cardiovascular-Measures.pdf
215. Book Text: *Gastroenterology* Link Associated with Text: https://www.cms.gov/Medicare/Quality-Initiatives-Patient-Assessment-Instruments/QualityMeasures/Downloads/Gastroenterology-Measures.pdf
216. Book Text: *HIV and Hepatitis C* Link Associated with Text: https://www.cms.gov/Medicare/Quality-Initiatives-Patient-Assessment-Instruments/QualityMeasures/Downloads/HIV-Hep-C-Core-Measures.pdf

217. Book Text: *Medical Oncology* Link Associated with Text:
https://www.cms.gov/Medicare/Quality-Initiatives-Patient-Assessment-Instruments/QualityMeasures/Downloads/Medical-Oncology-Measures.pdf
218. Book Text: *Obstetrics and Gynecology* Link Associated with Text:
https://www.cms.gov/Medicare/Quality-Initiatives-Patient-Assessment-Instruments/QualityMeasures/Downloads/OB-GYN-Measures.pdf
219. Book Text: *Orthopedics* Link Associated with Text:
https://www.cms.gov/Medicare/Quality-Initiatives-Patient-Assessment-Instruments/QualityMeasures/Downloads/Orthopedic-Measures.pdf
220. Book Text: *Pediatrics* Link Associated with Text:
https://www.cms.gov/Medicare/Quality-Initiatives-Patient-Assessment-Instruments/QualityMeasures/Downloads/Pediatric-Measures.pdf
221. Book Text: *(CAHPS) program* Link Associated with Text:
https://www.ahrq.gov/cahps/about-cahps/cahps-program/index.html
222. Book Text: *CAHPS surveys* Link Associated with Text:
https://www.ahrq.gov/cahps/surveys-guidance/index.html
223. Book Text: *HCAHPS* Link Associated with Text:
https://www.ahrq.gov/cahps/surveys-guidance/hospital/index.html
224. Book Text: *implemented by* Link Associated with Text:
https://www.hcahpsonline.org/en/
225. Book Text: *QPP* Link Associated with Text: https://qpp.cms.gov/
226. Book Text: *MACRA* Link Associated with Text:
https://www.cms.gov/Medicare/Quality-Initiatives-Patient-Assessment-Instruments/Value-Based-Programs/MACRA-MIPS-and-APMs/MACRA-MIPS-and-APMs.html
227. Book Text: *APMs* Link Associated with Text:
https://qpp.cms.gov/apms/overview?py=2019
228. Book Text: *Bundled Payments for Care Improvement Advanced Model (BPCI Advanced)* Link Associated with Text:
https://innovation.cms.gov/initiatives/bpci-advanced
229. Book Text: *Medicare Accountable Care Organization (ACO) Track 1+ Model* Link Associated with Text:
https://www.cms.gov/Medicare/Medicare-Fee-for-Service-Payment/sharedsavingsprogram/about.html
230. Book Text: *Next Generation ACO Model* Link Associated with Text:
https://innovation.cms.gov/initiatives/Next-Generation-ACO-Model/
231. Book Text: *Oncology Care Model (OCM) - Two-Sided Risk* Link Associated with Text: https://innovation.cms.gov/initiatives/oncology-care/
232. Book Text: *Comprehensive Care for Joint Replacement (CJR) Payment Model (Track 1- CEHRT)* Link Associated with Text:
https://innovation.cms.gov/initiatives/cjr
233. Book Text: *MIPS* Link Associated with Text:
https://qpp.cms.gov/mips/overview

234. Book Text: *Quality* Link Associated with Text: https://qpp.cms.gov/mips/explore-measures/quality-measures?py=2019#measures
235. Book Text: *Promoting Interoperability* Link Associated with Text: https://qpp.cms.gov/mips/explore-measures/promoting-interoperability?py=2019#measures
236. Book Text: *Improvement Activities* Link Associated with Text: https://qpp.cms.gov/mips/explore-measures/improvement-activities?py=2019#measures
237. Book Text: *Cost* Link Associated with Text: https://qpp.cms.gov/mips/explore-measures/cost?py=2019#measures
238. Book Text: *Video: What is the Scoring Methodology for the Merit-based Incentive Payment System?* Link Associated with Text: https://www.youtube.com/watch?v=OHOEQRo4qOs
239. Book Text: *Joint Commission programs* Link Associated with Text: https://www.jointcommission.org/specifications_manual_joint_commission_national_quality_core_measures.aspx
240. Book Text: *Performance Measurement* Link Associated with Text: https://www.jointcommission.org/performance_measurement.aspx
241. Book Text: *Accountability Measures* Link Associated with Text: https://www.jointcommission.org/accountability_measures.aspx
242. Book Text: *Leapfrog Group* Link Associated with Text: http://www.leapfroggroup.org/about
243. Book Text: *Hospital Survey* Link Associated with Text: http://www.leapfroggroup.org/survey-materials/survey-login-and-materials
244. Book Text: *Choosing the right hospital* Link Associated with Text: http://www.leapfroggroup.org/hospital-choice/choosing-right-hospital
245. Book Text: *Top Hospitals* Link Associated with Text: http://www.leapfroggroup.org/ratings-reports/top-hospitals
246. Book Text: *Hospital Compare* Link Associated with Text: https://www.medicare.gov/hospitalcompare/search.html
247. Book Text: *Measures and current data collection periods* Link Associated with Text: https://www.medicare.gov/hospitalcompare/Data/Data-Updated.html
248. Book Text: *Hospital Compare overall hospital rating* Link Associated with Text: https://www.medicare.gov/hospitalcompare/Data/Hospital-overall-ratings-calculation.html
249. Book Text: *Health Care Rankings* Link Associated with Text: https://health.usnews.com/health-care
250. Book Text: *Nursing Home Ranking* Link Associated with Text: https://health.usnews.com/best-nursing-homes
251. Book Text: *Yelp (Health)* Link Associated with Text: https://www.usnews.com/news/healthiest-communities/articles/2018-04-26/are-yelp-style-reviews-good-or-bad-for-us-health-care

252. Book Text: *RateMDs* Link Associated with Text:
https://www.ratemds.com/
253. Book Text: *Healthgrades* Link Associated with Text:
https://www.healthgrades.com/
254. Book Text: *Vitals* Link Associated with Text: https://www.vitals.com/
255. Book Text: *DATA.GOV* Link Associated with Text:
https://www.data.gov/
256. Book Text: *HealthData.gov* Link Associated with Text:
https://www.healthdata.gov/
257. Book Text: *Health IT Dashboard, Data* Link Associated with Text:
https://dashboard.healthit.gov/datadashboard/data.php
258. Book Text: *Centers for Disease Control and Prevention (CDC), Data
Access, Public-Use Data Files and Documentation* Link Associated with
Text: https://www.cdc.gov/nchs/data_access/ftp_data.htm
259. Book Text: *openFDA, Datasets* Link Associated with Text:
https://open.fda.gov/data/
260. Book Text: *Data.Medicare.gov* Link Associated with Text:
https://data.medicare.gov/
261. Book Text: *Oral Health Quality Improvement Initiative* Link Associated
with Text:
https://www.medicaid.gov/medicaid/benefits/dental/index.html
262. Book Text: *DQA* Link Associated with Text:
https://www.ada.org/en/science-research/dental-quality-alliance/dqa-
measure-activities/measures-medicaid-and-dental-plan-assessments
263. Book Text: *NQF2511* Link Associated with Text:
http://www.qualityforum.org/QPS/MeasureDetails.aspx?standardID=2511
&print=0&entityTypeID=1
264. Book Text: *NQF2528* Link Associated with Text:
http://www.qualityforum.org/QPS/MeasureDetails.aspx?standardID=2528
&print=0&entityTypeID=1
265. Book Text: *Dental Plan Survey* Link Associated with Text:
https://www.ahrq.gov/cahps/surveys-guidance/dental/index.html
266. Book Text: *was developed by* Link Associated with Text:
https://www.ahrq.gov/cahps/surveys-guidance/dental/about/Development-
of-the-Dental-Plan-Survey.html
267. Book Text: *AIR* Link Associated with Text: https://www.air.org/
268. Book Text: *TRICARE* Link Associated with Text:
https://www.tricare.mil/About
269. Book Text: *Video: Your Inner Fish: The Evolution of your Teeth* Link
Associated with Text:
https://www.youtube.com/watch?v=ohq3CoOKEoo
270. Book Text: *Practice Assessments* Link Associated with Text:
https://www.ada.org/en/science-research/dental-quality-alliance/dqa-
measure-activities/measures-practice-assessments

271. Book Text: *DQA Measure Activities* Link Associated with Text: https://www.ada.org/en/science-research/dental-quality-alliance/dqa-measure-activities

272. Book Text: *Yelp* Link Associated with Text: https://www.yelp.com/

273. Book Text: *RateMDs, Dentist* Link Associated with Text: https://www.ratemds.com/best-doctors/?specialty=dentist

274. Book Text: *Healthgrades, Find a Dentist* Link Associated with Text: https://www.healthgrades.com/dentistry-general-directory

275. Book Text: *Healthgrades, Find an Orthodontics Specialist* Link Associated with Text: https://www.healthgrades.com/orthodontics-directory

276. Book Text: *Vitals, Find a Dentist Near Me* Link Associated with Text: https://www.vitals.com/dentists

277. Book Text: *RankMyDentist* Link Associated with Text: http://www.rankmydentist.com/

278. Book Text: *American Dental Association (ADA), Health Policy Institute, Data Center* Link Associated with Text: https://www.ada.org/en/science-research/health-policy-institute/data-center

279. Book Text: *Oral Health Data* Link Associated with Text: https://www.cdc.gov/oralhealthdata/index.html

280. Book Text: *How to Find a Good Dentist* Link Associated with Text: https://health.usnews.com/health-care/patient-advice/articles/how-to-find-a-good-dentist

281. Book Text: *Measuring the Quality of Care* Link Associated with Text: https://www.agd.org/docs/default-source/policies-and-white-papers/impact-and-gd-articles/measuring-the-quality-of-care.pdf?sfvrsn=2

282. Book Text: *Measuring Up* Link Associated with Text: https://www.ncbi.nlm.nih.gov/pmc/articles/PMC4706780/

283. Book Text: *Clinical Performance Measures and Quality Improvement System Considerations for Dental Education* Link Associated with Text: http://www.jdentaled.org/content/81/3/347

284. Book Text: *Healthy People 2020: Oral Health* Link Associated with Text: https://www.healthypeople.gov/2020/topics-objectives/topic/oral-health

285. Book Text: *compounding* Link Associated with Text: https://www.pccarx.com/aboutus/whatiscompounding.aspx

286. Book Text: *compounding pharmacies* Link Associated with Text: https://en.wikipedia.org/wiki/Compounding#History

287. Book Text: *Merck* Link Associated with Text: https://www.merck.com/about/our-history/home.html

288. Book Text: *selling of alkaloids* Link Associated with Text: https://pharmaphorum.com/articles/a_history_of_the_pharmaceutical_industry/

289. Book Text: *Pfizer* Link Associated with Text: https://www.pfizer.com/about/history/all

290. Book Text: *Charles Pfizer* Link Associated with Text: https://en.wikipedia.org/wiki/Charles_Pfizer
291. Book Text: *Charles F. Erhart* Link Associated with Text: https://en.wikipedia.org/wiki/Charles_F._Erhart
292. Book Text: *santonin* Link Associated with Text: https://en.wikipedia.org/wiki/Santonin
293. Book Text: *CPPA* Link Associated with Text: https://www.pharmacypracticeaccredit.org/
294. Book Text: *Community Pharmacy Practice Accreditation* Link Associated with Text: https://www.pharmacypracticeaccredit.org/our-programs/community-pharmacy-practice-accreditation-program
295. Book Text: *Specialty Pharmacy Practice Accreditation* Link Associated with Text: https://www.pharmacypracticeaccredit.org/our-programs/specialty-pharmacy-practice-accreditation-program
296. Book Text: *Telehealth Pharmacy Practice Accreditation* Link Associated with Text: https://www.pharmacypracticeaccredit.org/our-programs/teleheath-pharmacy-practice-accreditation
297. Book Text: *ACHC* Link Associated with Text: https://www.achc.org/index.html
298. Book Text: *Pharmacy Accreditation* Link Associated with Text: https://www.achc.org/pharmacy.html
299. Book Text: *Compounding Pharmacy Accreditation* Link Associated with Text: https://www.achc.org/compounding-pharmacy.html
300. Book Text: *J.D. Power Healthcare Ratings* Link Associated with Text: https://www.jdpower.com/business/ratings/industry/healthcare
301. Book Text: *Chain Drug Store Pharmacy* Link Associated with Text: https://www.jdpower.com/business/ratings/study/U.S.-Pharmacy-Study-Brick-and-Mortar/4690ENG/Chain-Drug-Stores/2041
302. Book Text: *Mass Merchandisers Pharmacy* Link Associated with Text: https://www.jdpower.com/business/ratings/study/U.S.-Pharmacy-Study-Brick-and-Mortar/4690ENG/Mass-Merchandisers/2042
303. Book Text: *Supermarket Pharmacy* Link Associated with Text: https://www.jdpower.com/business/ratings/study/U.S.-Pharmacy-Study-Brick-and-Mortar/4690ENG/Supermarkets/2043
304. Book Text: *Mail Order Pharmacy* Link Associated with Text: https://www.jdpower.com/business/ratings/study/U.S.-Pharmacy-Study-Mail-Order/4691ENG
305. Book Text: *Healthgrades, Find a Pharmacist* Link Associated with Text: https://www.healthgrades.com/pharmacy-directory
306. Book Text: *RateMyPharmacy* Link Associated with Text: http://www.ratemypharmacy.com/
307. Book Text: *Bureau of Chemistry within the United States Department of Agriculture (USDA)* Link Associated with Text: https://www.fda.gov/AboutFDA/History/default.htm
308. Book Text: *drugs* Link Associated with Text: https://www.fda.gov/Drugs/default.htm

309. Book Text: *Drug Development Process* Link Associated with Text: https://www.fda.gov/forpatients/approvals/drugs/
310. Book Text: *Discovery and Development* Link Associated with Text: https://www.fda.gov/patients/drug-development-process/step-1-discovery-and-development
311. Book Text: *Preclinical Research* Link Associated with Text: https://www.fda.gov/patients/drug-development-process/step-2-preclinical-research
312. Book Text: *Clinical Research* Link Associated with Text: https://www.fda.gov/patients/drug-development-process/step-3-clinical-research
313. Book Text: *FDA Drug Review* Link Associated with Text: https://www.fda.gov/patients/drug-development-process/step-4-fda-drug-review
314. Book Text: *FDA Post-Market Drug Safety Monitoring* Link Associated with Text: https://www.fda.gov/patients/drug-development-process/step-5-fda-post-market-drug-safety-monitoring
315. Book Text: *clinical trials* Link Associated with Text: https://clinicaltrials.gov/
316. Book Text: *FDA Adverse Event Reporting System (FAERS)* Link Associated with Text: https://www.fda.gov/Drugs/GuidanceComplianceRegulatoryInformation/Surveillance/AdverseDrugEffects/default.htm
317. Book Text: *MedWatch: The FDA Safety Information and Adverse Event Reporting Program* Link Associated with Text: https://www.fda.gov/Safety/MedWatch/default.htm
318. Book Text: *Drugs@FDA: FDA Approved Drug Products* Link Associated with Text: https://www.accessdata.fda.gov/scripts/cder/daf/index.cfm
319. Book Text: *Orange Book* Link Associated with Text: https://www.fda.gov/Drugs/DevelopmentApprovalProcess/ucm079068.htm
320. Book Text: *Resources for Information on Approved Drugs* Link Associated with Text: https://www.fda.gov/Drugs/InformationOnDrugs/ApprovedDrugs/default.htm
321. Book Text: *Video: The Drug Discovery Process* Link Associated with Text: https://www.youtube.com/watch?v=DhxD6sVQEYc
322. Book Text: *right-to-try laws* Link Associated with Text: https://en.wikipedia.org/wiki/Right-to-try_law
323. Book Text: *Right-to-Try Act* Link Associated with Text: http://righttotry.org/rtt-faq/
324. Book Text: *are not FDA approved* Link Associated with Text: https://www.fda.gov/drugs/guidancecomplianceregulatoryinformation/pharmacycompounding/ucm339764.htm

325. Book Text: *WebMD Drugs and Medications* Link Associated with Text: https://www.webmd.com/drugs/2/index
326. Book Text: *DrugRatingz.com* Link Associated with Text: https://www.drugratingz.com/
327. Book Text: *Ask a Patient* Link Associated with Text: https://www.askapatient.com/
328. Book Text: *Iodine.com* Link Associated with Text: https://www.iodine.com/
329. Book Text: *Health Insurance Plan Ratings* Link Associated with Text: http://healthinsuranceratings.ncqa.org/2018/Default.aspx
330. Book Text: *Methodology* Link Associated with Text: https://www.ncqa.org/wp-content/uploads/2018/09/201808013_Health_Plan_Ratings_Methodology.pdf
331. Book Text: *HPA* Link Associated with Text: https://www.ncqa.org/programs/health-plans/health-plan-accreditation-hpa/
332. Book Text: *Health Plan Accreditation* Link Associated with Text: https://www.urac.org/programs/health-plan-accreditation
333. Book Text: *Plan Quality and Performance Ratings* Link Associated with Text: https://www.medicare.gov/find-a-plan/results/planresults/planratings/compare-plan-ratings.aspx?PlanType=MAPD&AspxAutoDetectCookieSupport=1#plan_rating_summary
334. Book Text: *Health Plan Quality Summary Rating* Link Associated with Text: https://www.medicare.gov/find-a-plan/staticpages/rating/planrating-help.aspx?termId=2019SS2
335. Book Text: *Video: CMS Star Ratings* Link Associated with Text: https://www.youtube.com/watch?v=fYnts1OOQsA
336. Book Text: *quality ratings* Link Associated with Text: https://www.healthcare.gov/quality-ratings/
337. Book Text: *Medicare Advantage Plans* Link Associated with Text: https://www.jdpower.com/business/ratings/study/Medicare-Advantage-Study/4190ENG
338. Book Text: *Vision Care Plans* Link Associated with Text: https://www.jdpower.com/business/ratings/study/Vision-Care-Satisfaction-Report/10011ENG
339. Book Text: *Medicaid and Dental Plan Assessments* Link Associated with Text: https://www.ada.org/en/science-research/dental-quality-alliance/dqa-measure-activities/measures-medicaid-and-dental-plan-assessments
340. Book Text: *Dental Plan Accreditation* Link Associated with Text: https://www.urac.org/programs/dental-plan-accreditation
341. Book Text: *Health Plan Dental Care Satisfaction* Link Associated with Text: https://www.jdpower.com/business/ratings/study/Dental-Care-Satisfaction-Study/10009ENG

342. Book Text: *Prescription Drug Plan Quality* Link Associated with Text: https://www.medicare.gov/find-a-plan/staticpages/rating/planrating-help.aspx?termId=2019SS1
343. Book Text: *Pharmacy Benefit Managers (PBMs)* Link Associated with Text: https://en.wikipedia.org/wiki/Pharmacy_benefit_management
344. Book Text: *PCMA* Link Associated with Text: https://www.pcmanet.org/about/
345. Book Text: *Express Scripts* Link Associated with Text: https://www.express-scripts.com/
346. Book Text: *Pharmacy Benefit Management Accreditation* Link Associated with Text: https://www.urac.org/programs/pharmacy-benefit-management-accreditation
347. Book Text: *Utilization Management Accreditation* Link Associated with Text: https://www.ncqa.org/programs/health-plans/utilization-management/
348. Book Text: *CVS Caremark* Link Associated with Text: https://www.caremark.com/wps/portal
349. Book Text: *has NCQA* Link Associated with Text: https://reportcards.ncqa.org/#/other-health-care-organization/Other_001G000001uwtCrIAI
350. Book Text: *is the PBM* Link Associated with Text: https://cvshealth.com/newsroom/press-releases/cvs-health-receives-ncqa-utilization-management-accreditation
351. Book Text: *Census Bureau Health Insurance Datasets* Link Associated with Text: https://www.census.gov/topics/health/health-insurance/data/datasets.html
352. Book Text: *CMS Health Insurance Exchange Public Use Files (Exchange PUFs)* Link Associated with Text: https://www.cms.gov/CCIIO/Resources/Data-Resources/marketplace-puf.html
353. Book Text: *Surgeon General's Office* Link Associated with Text: https://www.surgeongeneral.gov/
354. Book Text: *USPHS* Link Associated with Text: https://usphs.gov/
355. Book Text: *CDC* Link Associated with Text: https://www.cdc.gov/
356. Book Text: *are part of* Link Associated with Text: https://www.hhs.gov/about/agencies/hhs-agencies-and-offices/index.html
357. Book Text: *HHS* Link Associated with Text: https://www.hhs.gov/
358. Book Text: *state Department of Health or Department of Public Health* Link Associated with Text: https://www.cdc.gov/stltpublichealth/sitesgovernance/index.html
359. Book Text: *USPHS began* Link Associated with Text: https://www.surgeongeneral.gov/about/history/index.html
360. Book Text: *The mission* Link Associated with Text: https://www.surgeongeneral.gov/corps/index.html
361. Book Text: *who has a focus* Link Associated with Text: https://www.surgeongeneral.gov/priorities/index.html

362. Book Text: *Public Health Reports* Link Associated with Text:
https://journals.sagepub.com/home/phr
363. Book Text: *Opioids and Addiction* Link Associated with Text:
https://www.surgeongeneral.gov/priorities/index.html#opioids
364. Book Text: *Tobacco* Link Associated with Text:
https://www.surgeongeneral.gov/priorities/index.html#tobacco
365. Book Text: *Community Health and Economic Prosperity* Link
Associated with Text:
https://www.surgeongeneral.gov/priorities/index.html#tobacco
366. Book Text: *Health and National Security* Link Associated with Text:
https://www.surgeongeneral.gov/priorities/index.html#sec
367. Book Text: *Oral Health* Link Associated with Text:
https://www.surgeongeneral.gov/priorities/index.html#oral
368. Book Text: *Emerging Public Health Threats* Link Associated with Text:
https://www.surgeongeneral.gov/priorities/index.html#public
369. Book Text: *Video: Lessons learned from the center of America's opioid
epidemic* Link Associated with Text:
https://www.youtube.com/watch?v=W-CU5Ei9oUU
370. Book Text: *Communicable Disease Center* Link Associated with Text:
https://www.cdc.gov/about/history/index.html
371. Book Text: *current mission* Link Associated with Text:
https://www.cdc.gov/about/organization/cio.htm
372. Book Text: *National Health Initiatives, Strategies & Action Plans* Link
Associated with Text:
https://www.cdc.gov/stltpublichealth/strategy/index.html
373. Book Text: *Strategic Plan* Link Associated with Text:
https://www.cdc.gov/about/organization/strategic-framework/index.html
374. Book Text: *NPHII* Link Associated with Text:
https://www.cdc.gov/stltpublichealth/nphii/index.html
375. Book Text: *national voluntary accreditation* Link Associated with Text:
https://www.cdc.gov/stltpublichealth/accreditation/index.html
376. Book Text: *PHAB* Link Associated with Text:
https://www.phaboard.org/
377. Book Text: *collaborative effort to eliminate smallpox* Link Associated
with Text: http://www.who.int/features/2010/smallpox/en/
378. Book Text: *Just prior to efforts* Link Associated with Text:
https://en.wikipedia.org/wiki/History_of_smallpox
379. Book Text: *Smallpox: A Great and Terrible Scourge* Link Associated
with Text: http://www.nlm.nih.gov/exhibition/smallpox/index.html
380. Book Text: *Smallpox and Its Eradication* Link Associated with Text:
http://whqlibdoc.who.int/smallpox/9241561106.pdf
381. Book Text: *Global Alert and Response (GAR) – Smallpox* Link
Associated with Text:
http://www.who.int/csr/disease/smallpox/en/index.html

382. Book Text: *Control, elimination, eradication and re-emergence of infectious diseases: getting the message right* Link Associated with Text: http://www.who.int/bulletin/volumes/84/2/editorial10206html/en/
383. Book Text: *issues reports based* Link Associated with Text: https://www.surgeongeneral.gov/library/index.html
384. Book Text: *Data and Statistics* Link Associated with Text: https://www.cdc.gov/DataStatistics/
385. Book Text: *Public-Use Data Files and Documentation* Link Associated with Text: https://www.cdc.gov/nchs/data_access/ftp_data.htm
386. Book Text: *Interactive Data Tools and Query Systems* Link Associated with Text: https://www.cdc.gov/nchs/tools/index.htm
387. Book Text: *Performance Management and Quality Improvement* Link Associated with Text: https://www.cdc.gov/stltpublichealth/performance/index.html
388. Book Text: *Healthy People* Link Associated with Text: https://www.healthypeople.gov/
389. Book Text: *goals are* Link Associated with Text: https://www.healthypeople.gov/2020/About-Healthy-People
390. Book Text: *DATA2020* Link Associated with Text: https://www.healthypeople.gov/2020/data-search/
391. Book Text: *LHI* Link Associated with Text: https://www.healthypeople.gov/2020/leading-health-indicators/2020-LHI-Topics
392. Book Text: *Website Source of Quote* Link Associated with Text: https://www.hcahpsonline.org/en/#aboutthesurvey
393. Book Text: *invention of the flush toilet* Link Associated with Text: https://www.baus.org.uk/museum/164/the_flush_toilet
394. Book Text: *Sir John Harrington* Link Associated with Text: https://en.wikipedia.org/wiki/John_Harington_(writer)
395. Book Text: *The History of Sanitary Sewers* Link Associated with Text: https://www.sewerhistory.org/
396. Book Text: *Pondering the Privy: A History of Outhouses* Link Associated with Text: https://www.lancasterfarming.com/pondering-the-privy-a-history-of-outhouses/article_3f416eae-d0df-5d7f-9e70-3fcfb72a110a.html
397. Book Text: *WPA Privy (1935-1943)* Link Associated with Text: https://www.historycolorado.org/wpa-privy-1935-1943
398. Book Text: *Corning Museum of Glass* Link Associated with Text: https://www.cmog.org/
399. Book Text: *3,500 years of history* Link Associated with Text: https://www.cmog.org/collection/galleries/35-centuries-glass-galleries
400. Book Text: *jars used by druggists* Link Associated with Text: https://www.cmog.org/collection/search/druggist
401. Book Text: *scientific glass* Link Associated with Text: https://asgs-glass.org/what-is-scientific-glassblowing/

402. Book Text: *Video: The Corning Museum of Glass* Link Associated with Text: https://www.youtube.com/watch?v=JCMrSiXXEYQ
403. Book Text: *QDA MINER LITE* Link Associated with Text: https://provalisresearch.com/products/qualitative-data-analysis-software/freeware/
404. Book Text: *Coding Analysis Toolkit (CAT)* Link Associated with Text: https://cat.texifter.com/
405. Book Text: *Qualitative Research (QRJ)* Link Associated with Text: https://journals.sagepub.com/home/qrj
406. Book Text: *Qualitative Health Research (QHR)* Link Associated with Text: https://journals.sagepub.com/home/qhr
407. Book Text: *four levels* Link Associated with Text: https://en.wikipedia.org/wiki/Level_of_measurement
408. Book Text: *Stanley Smith Stevens* Link Associated with Text: https://en.wikipedia.org/wiki/Stanley_Smith_Stevens
409. Book Text: *On the Theory and Scales of Measurement* Link Associated with Text: http://science.sciencemag.org/content/103/2684/677
410. Book Text: *is different from that* Link Associated with Text: https://www.fahrenheittocelsius.com/
411. Book Text: *Excel* Link Associated with Text: https://products.office.com/en-us/excel
412. Book Text: *LibreOffice Calc* Link Associated with Text: https://www.libreoffice.org/discover/calc/
413. Book Text: *SAS* Link Associated with Text: https://www.sas.com/en_us/home.html
414. Book Text: *The R Project for Statistical Computing* Link Associated with Text: https://www.r-project.org/
415. Book Text: *ArcGIS* Link Associated with Text: https://www.arcgis.com/index.html
416. Book Text: *data to be the foundation* Link Associated with Text: https://www.hrsa.gov/sites/default/files/quality/toolbox/508pdfs/qualityimprovement.pdf
417. Book Text: *Such a document* Link Associated with Text: https://www.icpsr.umich.edu/icpsrweb/content/shared/ICPSR/faqs/what-is-a-codebook.html
418. Book Text: *Medicare Current Beneficiary Survey (MCBS) Data Documentation and Codebooks* Link Associated with Text: https://www.cms.gov/Research-Statistics-Data-and-Systems/Research/MCBS/Codebooks.html
419. Book Text: *NHDS - Downloadable documentation via ftp* Link Associated with Text: ftp://ftp.cdc.gov/pub/Health_Statistics/NCHS/Dataset_Documentation/NHDS
420. Book Text: *NHAMCS, 1992-2016* Link Associated with Text: ftp://ftp.cdc.gov/pub/Health_Statistics/NCHS/Dataset_Documentation/NHAMCS

421. Book Text: *Appendix C. Data Dictionary* Link Associated with Text:
https://www.ahrq.gov/research/findings/final-reports/ssi/ssiapc.html
422. Book Text: *re3data.org* Link Associated with Text:
https://www.re3data.org/
423. Book Text: *Open Access Directory* Link Associated with Text:
http://oad.simmons.edu/oadwiki/Data_repositories
424. Book Text: *HMCA* Link Associated with Text:
https://www.icpsr.umich.edu/icpsrweb/content/HMCA/index.html
425. Book Text: *ICPSR* Link Associated with Text:
https://www.icpsr.umich.edu/icpsrweb/
426. Book Text: *Guide to Social Science Data Preparation and Archiving*
Link Associated with Text:
http://www.icpsr.umich.edu/files/ICPSR/access/dataprep.pdf
427. Book Text: *ICPSR Electronic Data Deposit Form* Link Associated with
Text: http://www.icpsr.umich.edu/files/deposit/ICPSR-deposit-form-
sample.pdf
428. Book Text: *Video: ICPSR 101: Why Should I Cite Data?* Link
Associated with Text: https://www.youtube.com/watch?v=jiCZKV-alC0
429. Book Text: *Data - Open Access Journal* Link Associated with Text:
https://www.mdpi.com/journal/data
430. Book Text: *Data-In-Brief Journal* Link Associated with Text:
https://www.journals.elsevier.com/data-in-brief
431. Book Text: *Scientific Data Journal* Link Associated with Text:
https://www.nature.com/sdata/
432. Book Text: *Create a Codebook* Link Associated with Text:
http://www.ddialliance.org/training/getting-started-new-content/create-a-
codebook
433. Book Text: *Codebook Cookbook* Link Associated with Text:
http://www.medicine.mcgill.ca/epidemiology/joseph/pbelisle/CodebookC
ookbook/CodebookCookbook.pdf
434. Book Text: *How to Make a Data Dictionary* Link Associated with Text:
http://help.osf.io/m/bestpractices/l/618767-how-to-make-a-data-dictionary
435. Book Text: *Documenting Data* Link Associated with Text:
http://libguides.mst.edu/c.php?g=335446&p=2257031
436. Book Text: *Data Documentation and Metadata* Link Associated with
Text: https://data.library.arizona.edu/data-management-tips/data-
documentation-and-metadata
437. Book Text: *Qualitative Research Design* Link Associated with Text:
https://researchrundowns.com/qual/qualitative-research-design/
438. Book Text: *Qualitative methods in research on healthcare quality* Link
Associated with Text: https://qualitysafety.bmj.com/content/11/2/148
439. Book Text: *Guidance for Measure Testing and Evaluating Scientific
Acceptability of Measure Properties* Link Associated with Text:
http://www.qualityforum.org/Measuring_Performance/Improving_NQF_P
rocess/Measure_Testing_Task_Force_Final_Report.aspx

440. Book Text: *surveys used for quality* Link Associated with Text: http://asq.org/learn-about-quality/data-collection-analysis-tools/overview/survey.html

441. Book Text: *sampling strategies used for quality* Link Associated with Text: https://www.isixsigma.com/tools-templates/sampling-data/basic-sampling-strategies-sample-vs-population-data/

442. Book Text: *Random sampling* Link Associated with Text: https://en.wikipedia.org/wiki/Simple_random_sample

443. Book Text: *Random Number Generator (RNG)* Link Associated with Text: https://stattrek.com/statistics/random-number-generator.aspx

444. Book Text: *Stratified random sampling* Link Associated with Text: http://asq.org/learn-about-quality/data-collection-analysis-tools/overview/stratification.html

445. Book Text: *Systematic sampling* Link Associated with Text: http://www.businessdictionary.com/definition/systematic-sampling.html

446. Book Text: *confidence level* Link Associated with Text: https://stattrek.com/statistics/dictionary.aspx?definition=confidence_level

447. Book Text: *confidence interval* Link Associated with Text: https://stattrek.com/statistics/dictionary.aspx?definition=confidence_interval

448. Book Text: *margin of error* Link Associated with Text: https://stattrek.com/statistics/dictionary.aspx?definition=margin%20of%20error

449. Book Text: *online sample size generator* Link Associated with Text: https://www.qualtrics.com/blog/calculating-sample-size/

450. Book Text: *classic, true experimental design* Link Associated with Text: https://cirt.gcu.edu/research/developmentresources/research_ready/experimental/design_types

451. Book Text: *quasi-experimental designs* Link Associated with Text: https://socialresearchmethods.net/kb/destypes.php

452. Book Text: *Design of Experiments (DOE)* Link Associated with Text: http://asq.org/learn-about-quality/data-collection-analysis-tools/overview/design-of-experiments.html

453. Book Text: *Ronald Fisher* Link Associated with Text: https://en.wikipedia.org/wiki/Ronald_Fisher

454. Book Text: *Design of Experiments* Link Associated with Text: https://www.medicine.mcgill.ca/epidemiology/hanley/tmp/Mean-Quantile/DesignofExperimentsCh-III.pdf

455. Book Text: *On the "Probable Error" of a Coefficient of Correlation Deduced from a Small Sample* Link Associated with Text: https://digital.library.adelaide.edu.au/dspace/handle/2440/15169

456. Book Text: *Fisher's z-distribution* Link Associated with Text: https://en.wikipedia.org/wiki/Fisher%27s_z-distribution

457. Book Text: *F-distribution* Link Associated with Text: https://en.wikipedia.org/wiki/F-distribution

458. *Statistical Methods for Research Workers.*

459. Book Text: *Understanding Design of Experiments* Link Associated with Text: https://www.qualitydigest.com/inside/quality-insider-article/understanding-design-experiments.html

460. Book Text: *What Is Design of Experiments (DOE)?* Link Associated with Text: http://asq.org/learn-about-quality/data-collection-analysis-tools/overview/design-of-experiments.html

461. Book Text: *Introduction to Design of Experiments (DOE)* Link Associated with Text: https://quality-one.com/doe/

462. Book Text: *Design of Experiments – A Primer* Link Associated with Text: https://www.isixsigma.com/tools-templates/design-of-experiments-doe/design-experiments-%E2%90%93-primer/

463. Book Text: *Experimental and Quasi-Experimental Designs for Research* Link Associated with Text: https://www.amazon.com/Experimental-Quasi-Experimental-Designs-Research-Campbell-ebook/dp/B014WQS2SY/ref=mt_kindle?_encoding=UTF8&me=

464. Book Text: *A First Course in Probability* Link Associated with Text: https://www.pearson.com/us/higher-education/program/Ross-First-Course-in-Probability-A-9th-Edition/PGM110742.html

465. Book Text: *History of Probability* Link Associated with Text: http://en.wikipedia.org/wiki/History_of_probability

466. Book Text: *SAGE Research Methods* Link Associated with Text: http://methods.sagepub.com/

467. Book Text: *Tests of Change: Simulated Design of Experiments in Healthcare Delivery* Link Associated with Text: https://www.psqh.com/analysis/tests-of-change/

468. Book Text: *DOE Use in the Health Care Industry* Link Associated with Text: http://qualityamerica.com/LSS-Knowledge-Center/designedexperiments/doe_use_in_the_health_care_industry.php

469. Book Text: *National Institutes of Health (NIH), Rigor and Responsibility* Link Associated with Text: https://www.nih.gov/research-training/rigor-reproducibility

470. Book Text: *Food and Drug Administration (FDA) Drug Study Designs, Information Sheet* Link Associated with Text: https://www.fda.gov/regulatory-information/search-fda-guidance-documents/drug-study-designs

471. Book Text: *FAQ: How and Why We Rank and Rate Hospitals* Link Associated with Text: https://health.usnews.com/health-care/best-hospitals/articles/faq-how-and-why-we-rank-and-rate-hospitals

472. Book Text: *Methodology: US News & World Report 2018-2019 Best Hospitals Specialty Rankings* Link Associated with Text: https://www.usnews.com/static/documents/health/best-hospitals/BH_Methodology_2018-19.pdf

473. Book Text: *overall hospital star* Link Associated with Text: https://www.medicare.gov/hospitalcompare/About/Hospital-overall-ratings.html

474. Book Text: *Overall Hospital Ratings, Methodology* Link Associated with Text: https://www.qualitynet.org/dcs/ContentServer?c=Page&pagename=QnetPublic%2FPage%2FQnetTier3&cid=1228775957165

475. Book Text: *CMS star ratings disproportionately benefit specialty hospitals, data show* Link Associated with Text: https://www.modernhealthcare.com/article/20180314/NEWS/180319952

476. Book Text: *3 Reasons CMS Star Ratings Are Misleading* Link Associated with Text: https://www.healthleadersmedia.com/strategy/3-reasons-cms-star-ratings-are-misleading

477. Book Text: *CMS Star Ratings Met with Criticism in Academic Medicine Community* Link Associated with Text: https://news.aamc.org/patient-care/article/cms-star-ratings-criticism-academic-med-community/

478. Book Text: *Three top criticisms against CMS' overall hospital star ratings* Link Associated with Text: http://www.managedhealthcareexecutive.com/hospitals-providers/three-top-criticisms-against-cms-overall-hospital-star-ratings

479. Book Text: *Patient Characteristics and Differences in Hospital Readmission Rates* Link Associated with Text: https://jamanetwork.com/journals/jamainternalmedicine/fullarticle/2434813#ioi150078r27

480. Book Text: *CMS star ratings criticized for ignoring socioeconomic factors* Link Associated with Text: https://www.healthexec.com/topics/quality/cms-star-ratings-criticized-ignoring-socioeconomic-factors

481. Book Text: *My Favorite Slide: Why Five-Star Hospitals May Be More Closely Related to Five-Star Restaurants than Innate Quality* Link Associated with Text: https://catalyst.nejm.org/five-star-hospitals-five-star-restaurants/

482. Book Text: *SAS – Industries – Health Care Analytics* Link Associated with Text: https://www.sas.com/en_us/industry/health-care-providers.html/

483. Book Text: *IBM SPSS Software* Link Associated with Text: https://www.ibm.com/analytics/spss-statistics-software

484. Book Text: *History of Statistics* Link Associated with Text: http://en.wikipedia.org/wiki/History_of_statistics

485. Book Text: *ESRI – Industries – Health and Human Services* Link Associated with Text: https://www.esri.com/en-us/industries/health/overview

486. Book Text: *National Center for Health Statistics (NCHS) Data Visualization Gallery* Link Associated with Text: https://blogs.cdc.gov/nchs-data-visualization/

487. Book Text: *GIS and Public Health at CDC* Link Associated with Text: https://www.cdc.gov/gis/index.htm

488. Book Text: *Principles of Epidemiology in Public Health Practice* Link Associated with Text:
https://www.cdc.gov/csels/dsepd/ss1978/index.html
489. Book Text: *Discovering Statistics Using R* Link Associated with Text:
https://us.sagepub.com/en-us/nam/discovering-statistics-using-r/book236067
490. Book Text: *Computational Handbook of Statistics* Link Associated with Text: https://www.amazon.com/Computational-Handbook-Statistics-James-Bruning/dp/0673990850/ref=sr_1_1?ie=UTF8&qid=1490068189&sr=8-1&keywords=computational+handbook+of+statistics
491. Book Text: *Spatial Statistics Journal* Link Associated with Text:
https://www.journals.elsevier.com/spatial-statistics
492. Book Text: *American Statistical Association (ASA)* Link Associated with Text: http://www.amstat.org/
493. Book Text: *Video: The beauty of data visualization* Link Associated with Text: https://www.youtube.com/watch?v=pLqjQ55tz-U
494. Book Text: *Kaoru Ishikawa* Link Associated with Text:
https://asq.org/about-asq/honorary-members/ishikawa
495. Book Text: *The Quality Toolbox* Link Associated with Text:
https://asq.org/quality-press/display-item?item=H1224
496. Book Text: *causes be organized* Link Associated with Text:
497. Book Text: *Five Whys Analysis* Link Associated with Text:
https://quality-one.com/5-why-5-how/
498. Book Text: *provides the following example* Link Associated with Text:
https://www.cms.gov/Medicare/Provider-Enrollment-and-Certification/QAPI/downloads/FiveWhys.pdf
499. Book Text: *Fishbone Template, Word* Link Associated with Text:
https://www.isixsigma.com/images/stories/migrated/downloads/fishbone_template.doc
500. Book Text: *How to Create a Fishbone Diagram in Word* Link Associated with Text: https://www.lucidchart.com/blog/how-to-create-a-fishbone-diagram-in-Word
501. Book Text: *Fishbone Template, Excel* Link Associated with Text:
https://www.isixsigma.com/images/stories/migrated/downloads/fishbone_template.xls
502. Book Text: *Fishbone (Cause & Effect Diagram) Excel Template* Link Associated with Text: http://asq.org/sixsigma/tools-exchange/docs/fishbone-cause-effect-diagram.xls
503. Book Text: *Fishbone Diagram Template in Excel* Link Associated with Text: https://www.lucidchart.com/pages/fishbone/fishbone-diagram-excel-template
504. Book Text: *How to Use the Fishbone Tool for Root Cause Analysis* Link Associated with Text: https://www.cms.gov/medicare/provider-enrollment-and-certification/qapi/downloads/fishbonerevised.pdf

505. Book Text: *CMS Process Tool Framework* Link Associated with Text: https://www.cms.gov/Medicare/Provider-Enrollment-and-Certification/QAPI/Downloads/ProcessToolFramework.pdf
506. Book Text: *QAPI* Link Associated with Text: https://www.cms.gov/Medicare/Provider-Enrollment-and-Certification/QAPI/qapitools.html
507. Book Text: *Minnesota Department of Health, Fishbone Diagram* Link Associated with Text: https://www.health.state.mn.us/communities/practice/resources/phqitoolbox/fishbone.html
508. Book Text: *Improhealth Collaborative, Fishbone Diagram* Link Associated with Text: http://www.improhealth.org/fileadmin/Documents/Improvement_Tools/Fishbone_diagram.pdf
509. Book Text: *Immunization Quality Improvement Project* Link Associated with Text: http://media.khi.org/news/documents/2009/05/19/1110-WestLongStoryboard.pdf
510. Book Text: *Using a Fishbone Diagram to Assess and Remedy Barriers to Cervical Cancer Screening in Your Healthcare Setting* Link Associated with Text: https://aidsetc.org/sites/default/files/resources_files/fishbone.ppt
511. Book Text: *Video: Fishbone Diagram* Link Associated with Text: https://www.youtube.com/watch?v=2rLB-1z9cPY
512. Book Text: *Fishbone (Ishikawa) Diagram* Link Associated with Text: http://asq.org/learn-about-quality/cause-analysis-tools/overview/fishbone.html
513. Book Text: *Fishbone Diagram Tutorial* Link Associated with Text: https://www.lucidchart.com/pages/fishbone/fishbone-diagram-tutorial
514. Book Text: *The Cause and Effect (a.k.a. Fishbone) Diagram* Link Associated with Text: https://www.isixsigma.com/tools-templates/cause-effect/cause-and-effect-aka-fishbone-diagram/
515. Book Text: *contain identifying information* Link Associated with Text: https://en.wikipedia.org/wiki/Check_sheet
516. Book Text: *Check Sheet* Link Associated with Text: https://www.health.state.mn.us/communities/practice/resources/phqitoolbox/checksheet.html
517. Book Text: *ASQ Check Sheet* Link Associated with Text:
518. Book Text: *Using Check Sheets to Improve Data Analysis* Link Associated with Text: https://www.qualitydigest.com/print/8318
519. Book Text: *defines a control chart* Link Associated with Text: http://asq.org/learn-about-quality/data-collection-analysis-tools/overview/control-chart.html
520. Book Text: *UCL and LCL are calculated* Link Associated with Text: https://sixsigmabasics.com/control-chart.html
521. Book Text: *standard deviations* Link Associated with Text: https://en.wikipedia.org/wiki/Standard_deviation

522. Book Text: *development of the control chart* Link Associated with Text: https://en.wikipedia.org/wiki/Control_chart
523. Book Text: *Walter Andrew Shewhart* Link Associated with Text: https://en.wikipedia.org/wiki/Walter_A._Shewhart
524. Book Text: *SPC* Link Associated with Text: https://quality-one.com/spc/
525. Book Text: *ISIXSIGMA* Link Associated with Text: https://www.isixsigma.com/ask-dr-mikel-harry/ask-tools-techniques/what-difference-between-spc-and-sqc/
526. Book Text: *Video: Honda Statistical Process Control* Link Associated with Text: https://www.youtube.com/watch?v=Sdj-8ZBYYmo
527. Book Text: *Common types of control charts* Link Associated with Text: https://www.isixsigma.com/tools-templates/control-charts/a-guide-to-control-charts/
528. Book Text: *Infinity QS* Link Associated with Text: https://www.infinityqs.com/industry/medical-pharmaceuticals
529. Book Text: *PQ Systems* Link Associated with Text: https://www.pqsystems.com/quality-solutions/statistical-process-control/SQCpack/
530. Book Text: *Control Chart Template, Excel* Link Associated with Text: http://asq.org/learn-about-quality/data-collection-analysis-tools/overview/asq-control-chart.xls
531. Book Text: *QI Macros* Link Associated with Text: https://www.qimacros.com/control-chart/
532. Book Text: *Statistical Process Control: Possible Uses to Monitor and Evaluate Patient-Centered Medical Home Models* Link Associated with Text: https://pcmh.ahrq.gov/page/statistical-process-controlpossible-uses-monitor-and-evaluate-patient-centered-medical-home
533. Book Text: *Application of statistical process control in healthcare improvement: systematic review* Link Associated with Text: https://www.researchgate.net/publication/5930807_Application_of_statistical_process_control_in_healthcare_improvement_systematic_review
534. Book Text: *Statistical process control as a tool for research and health care improvement* Link Associated with Text: http://www.ihi.org/resources/Pages/Publications/Statisticalprocesscontrolasatoolforresearchandhealthcareimprovement.aspx
535. Book Text: *Statistical Process Control* Link Associated with Text: https://healthit.ahrq.gov/health-it-tools-and-resources/evaluation-resources/workflow-assessment-health-it-toolkit/all-workflow-tools/statistical-process-control
536. Book Text: *Control Chart* Link Associated with Text: https://www.health.state.mn.us/communities/practice/resources/phqitoolbox/controlchart.html
537. Book Text: *Statistical Process Control for Health Care* Link Associated with Text: https://www.qualitydigest.com/june08/articles/03_article.shtml

538. Book Text: *histogram* Link Associated with Text: https://en.wikipedia.org/wiki/Histogram
539. Book Text: *Excel includes* Link Associated with Text: https://support.office.com/en-us/article/create-a-histogram-in-excel-85680173-064b-4024-b39d-80f17ff2f4e8
540. Book Text: *Excel template* Link Associated with Text: http://asq.org/learn-about-quality/data-collection-analysis-tools/overview/data-point-histogram.xls
541. Book Text: *ASQ states* Link Associated with Text: http://asqservicequality.org/glossary/histogram/
542. Book Text: *histogram analysis* Link Associated with Text: http://asq.org/learn-about-quality/data-collection-analysis-tools/overview/histogram.html
543. Book Text: *Typical Histogram Shapes and What They Mean* Link Associated with Text: http://asq.org/learn-about-quality/data-collection-analysis-tools/overview/histogram2.html
544. Book Text: *states that* Link Associated with Text: http://asq.org/learn-about-quality/cause-analysis-tools/overview/pareto.html
545. Book Text: *Video: Pareto Chart* Link Associated with Text: https://www.youtube.com/watch?v=pLWBG_CZ4ZY
546. Book Text: *as a chart option* Link Associated with Text: https://support.office.com/en-us/article/create-a-pareto-chart-a1512496-6dba-4743-9ab1-df5012972856
547. Book Text: *Pareto chart Excel template* Link Associated with Text: http://asq.org/learn-about-quality/data-collection-analysis-tools/overview/data-analysis.xls
548. Book Text: *When to Use a Pareto Chart* Link Associated with Text: http://blog.minitab.com/blog/understanding-statistics/when-to-use-a-pareto-chart
549. Book Text: *What is a Pareto Chart?* Link Associated with Text: https://www.health.state.mn.us/communities/practice/resources/phqitoolbox/pareto.html
550. Book Text: *Purpose of a Pareto Chart* Link Associated with Text: https://www.isixsigma.com/tools-templates/graphical-analysis-charts/pareto-chart-bar-chart-histogram-and-pareto-principle-8020-rule/
551. Book Text: *Pareto Charts* Link Associated with Text: https://www.usaidassist.org/resources/pareto-charts
552. Book Text: *Pareto Diagram* Link Associated with Text: https://www.health.state.mn.us/communities/practice/resources/phqitoolbox/docs/paretodiagram_ihi.pdf
553. Book Text: *scatter diagram* Link Associated with Text: https://en.wikipedia.org/wiki/Scatter_plot
554. Book Text: *ASQ states that* Link Associated with Text: http://asq.org/learn-about-quality/cause-analysis-tools/overview/scatter.html

555. Book Text: *includes the scatter diagram* Link Associated with Text: https://support.office.com/en-us/article/present-your-data-in-a-scatter-chart-or-a-line-chart-4570a80f-599a-4d6b-a155-104a9018b86e

556. Book Text: *scatter diagram Excel template* Link Associated with Text: http://asq.org/sixsigma/tools-exchange/docs/scatter-diagram.xls

557. Book Text: *Scatter Plot* Link Associated with Text: https://www.health.state.mn.us/communities/practice/resources/phqitoolbox/scatterplot.html

558. Book Text: *Scatter Diagram, MathWorld* Link Associated with Text: http://mathworld.wolfram.com/ScatterDiagram.html

559. Book Text: *stratified sampling* Link Associated with Text: https://en.wikipedia.org/wiki/Stratified_sampling

560. Book Text: *defined by ASQ* Link Associated with Text: http://asq.org/learn-about-quality/data-collection-analysis-tools/overview/stratification.html

561. Book Text: *illustrating stratification* Link Associated with Text: http://asq.org/sixsigma/tools-exchange/docs/stratification-diagram-template.xls

562. Book Text: *Stratification Leads to Specialized Improvements* Link Associated with Text: https://www.isixsigma.com/tools-templates/sampling-data/stratification-leads-specialized-improvements/

563. Book Text: *Stratification* Link Associated with Text: https://www.isixsigma.com/dictionary/stratification/

564. Book Text: *Medicinal plants* Link Associated with Text: https://en.wikipedia.org/wiki/Medicinal_plants

565. Book Text: *Nikolai Ivanovich Vavilov* Link Associated with Text: https://en.wikipedia.org/wiki/Nikolai_Vavilov

566. Book Text: *Siege of Leningrad* Link Associated with Text: https://en.wikipedia.org/wiki/Siege_of_Leningrad

567. Book Text: *accumulated seeds* Link Associated with Text: https://www.rbth.com/blogs/2014/05/12/the_men_who_starved_to_death_to_save_the_worlds_seeds_35135

568. Book Text: *Institute still exists* Link Associated with Text: https://phys.org/news/2017-01-russia-vavilov-guardian-world-lost.html

569. Book Text: *Facts About the Global Seed Vault* Link Associated with Text: https://www.livescience.com/56247-global-seed-vault.html

570. Book Text: *Svalbard Global Seed Vault* Link Associated with Text: https://www.croptrust.org/our-work/svalbard-global-seed-vault/

571. Book Text: *Wikipedia, Global Seed Vault* Link Associated with Text: https://en.wikipedia.org/wiki/Svalbard_Global_Seed_Vault

572. Book Text: *United States Botanic Garden* Link Associated with Text: https://www.usbg.gov/

573. Book Text: *Video: United States Botanic Garden* Link Associated with Text: https://www.youtube.com/watch?v=HpSbhezAVTU

574. Book Text: *Video: LibreOffice-Calc, OpenOffice-Calc, Excel Tutorial -- A first Look* Link Associated with Text: https://www.youtube.com/watch?v=HdOLxR_NlrQ
575. Book Text: *Video: Libre Office - Calc, Open Office - Calc, Excel Tutorial - Charts Data Series* Link Associated with Text: https://www.youtube.com/watch?v=MEUuwq7FS7k
576. Book Text: *Video: 20 Principles for Good Spreadsheet Practice* Link Associated with Text: https://www.youtube.com/watch?v=UK_YpZBB02Y
577. Book Text: *1942: Navajo Code Talkers* Link Associated with Text: https://www.intelligence.gov/index.php/people/barrier-breakers-in-history/453-navajo-code-talkers
578. Book Text: *Codetalker* Link Associated with Text: http://www.americanindiansource.com/codetalker.html
579. Book Text: *Navajo Windtalkers* Link Associated with Text: http://math.ucsd.edu/~crypto/Projects/RobertoSandoval/NavajoWindtalkers.pdf
580. Book Text: *National Cryptologic Museum* Link Associated with Text: https://www.nsa.gov/about/cryptologic-heritage/museum/
581. Book Text: *Department of Health and Human Services (HHS): Encryption* Link Associated with Text: https://www.hhs.gov/hipaa/for-professionals/faq/encryption/index.html
582. Book Text: *Encryption vs. Cryptography – What is the Difference* Link Associated with Text: https://www.brighthub.com/computing/enterprise-security/articles/65254.aspx
583. Book Text: *Basic cryptology concepts* Link Associated with Text: https://www.ibm.com/developerworks/tivoli/tutorials/s-crypto/s-crypto.html
584. Book Text: *Video: Decoding the National Cryptologic Museum* Link Associated with Text: https://www.youtube.com/watch?v=pses-io-Obw
585. Book Text: *National Parks of the United States* Link Associated with Text: https://www.nps.gov/findapark/index.htm
586. Book Text: *Zion National Park* Link Associated with Text: https://www.nps.gov/zion/index.htm
587. Book Text: *Video: Angel's Landing - Scariest Hike in America? Steep Drop Off* Link Associated with Text: https://www.youtube.com/watch?v=jy6K0KoMrco

www.ingramcontent.com/pod-product-compliance
Lightning Source LLC
Chambersburg PA
CBHW041221270326
41932CB00006B/43